THE THOMISTIC CONCEPTION
OF AN INTERNATIONAL SOCIETY

THE CATHOLIC UNIVERSITY OF AMERICA
PHILOSOPHICAL STUDIES
VOLUME 70

THE THOMISTIC CONCEPTION OF AN INTERNATIONAL SOCIETY

A Dissertation

SUBMITTED TO THE FACULTY OF THE SCHOOL OF PHILOSOPHY OF THE
CATHOLIC UNIVERSITY OF AMERICA IN PARTIAL FULFILLMENT
OF REQUIREMENTS FOR THE DEGREE OF
DOCTOR OF PHILOSOPHY

BY

GERALD FRANCIS BENKERT, O.S.B., M.A.

OF

ST. MEINRAD'S ABBEY

ST. MEINRAD, INDIANA

THE CATHOLIC UNIVERSITY OF AMERICA PRESS
WASHINGTON, D. C.
1942

IMPRIMI POTEST:

✝ IGNATIUS ESSER, O.S.B.
Abbas Monasterii Sancti Meinradi

NIHIL OBSTAT:

IGNATIUS SMITH, O.P., PH.D.
Censor Deputatus

IMPRIMATUR:

✝ JOSEPH E. RITTER, D.D.
Episcopus Indianapolitanus

INDIANAPOLI, IND., DIE XXVII JUNII, 1942

PRINTED BY
THE ABBEY PRESS
ST. MEINRAD, INDIANA

JESU CHRISTO
UNIVERSORUM REGI
FAMILIAE GENTIUM CAPITI
JUSTITIAE ET AMORIS ET PACIS
PRINCIPI

TABLE OF CONTENTS

vii

PREFACE

In his Encyclical Letter *Studiorum Ducem,* issued June 29, 1923, on the sixth centenary of the canonization of St. Thomas Aquinas, Pope Pius XI stated that the teaching of this greatest of Scholastic Philosophers and Doctor of the Church contains the doctrinal basis for a true international society.

> Thus in the second part of the *Summa Theologica* we may find chapters which are unsurpassed on such subjects as the power and rights of the father, the so-called domestic rights, on the rights of the state and of the nation, on natural rights and international law, on peace, war, justice, and property rights, on laws and their observance, on the duty of working for our individual welfare and for the welfare of the public. All these subjects he treats not only from the side of the natural but of the supernatural order as well. If these teachings of his were exactly and religious observed by all men, both in their public and private lives, nothing else would be required to bring about among men that "peace of Christ in the Kingdom of Christ" for which the whole world so ardently sighs. There is this further reason that it is most desirable that we understand and appreciate more and more the teachings of St. Thomas on the rights of nations and on the laws which regulate the relations of peoples with one another, since these doctrines contain the foundations for a true Society of Nations.[1]

The subject and the purpose of this dissertation are well expressed in these words of Pope Pius XI. The following pages are an attempt to construct a Thomistic concept of international society—a conception derived from the fundamental principles of the moral, social, and political philosophy of St. Thomas Aquinas. It is true that a complete and fully developed outline of such a society is not to be found explicitly in the writings of St. Thomas. Such is not the meaning of Pope Pius' statement. But these writings do contain sound philosophical principles which, when fully

---

[1] Pope Pius XI, Encyclical Letter *Studiorum Ducem.*

developed and elaborated, form a solid basis for the construction of a true international society.

It was a disciple of St. Thomas who first extended explicitly and professedly the principles of the Master to the field of international relations, and in so doing drew up, at least in general form, the outline of an international society on a world-wide scale—a society which should ultimately embrace all peoples organized into political communities or states. This disciple is Francis de Vitoria, who, three centuries after the time of St. Thomas, inaugurated the great Spanish revival of Thomistic philosophy and theology, and who, because of his application of the principles of this philosophy to the field of international relations, has been officially acclaimed by the Seventh International Conference of American States as "the professor of Salamanca who, in the sixteenth century, established the foundations of modern international law."[2]   In his treatises on the principles of international law, Francis de Vitoria at the same time indicated his conception of a universal society of nations or states implied in and underlying this very law of nations. In developing a Thomistic conception of an international society, therefore, the lead of Francis de Vitoria will be closely followed. The works of St. Thomas Aquinas and the writings of Francis de Vitoria will supply the two main sources of the material for this study. To these must be added the writings of a number of contemporary scholars and students of Aquinas and Vitoria who have contributed to the formation of a definite Thomistic conception of international society. But before proceeding to this work itself, several important points must be noted.

In the first place, the subject and scope of this dissertation is limited to a Thomistic conception of an international society, with its underlying principles, functions and requirements; it is not a treatise on international law. Con-

---

[2] Resolution of the Seventh International Conference of American States, quoted from Scott, James Brown, *The Catholic Conception of International Law*, Washington: Georgetown University Press, 1934, p. VII.

sequently it does not pertain to the field of jurisprudence or international law; it belongs solely and properly to the field of moral, social, and political philosophy. International law will be mentioned only in connection with international society as one of its essential functions and requirements. Hence, if but passing reference is made to men who are famous as pioneers in the science of international law, such as Grotius and Gentili, it is because they lie outside the scope of this treatise.

Secondly, it should be observed that it is with the philosophical conception of international society that we are properly concerned in these pages, not with the practical organization or the construction of the governmental machinery of such a society. Consequently, no proposals will be made nor any suggestions offered for the practical construction of a Society of States or League of Nations, for such is the proper work of political scientists, jurists, and statesmen. Our task is rather to develop and elaborate the philosophical principles upon which such a society can be firmly erected. In this connection, it should likewise be mentioned that these philosophical principles are the principles of the natural order, based on the natural law, as developed in the philosophical system of St. Thomas Aquinas. However it should not be inferred from this that the truths of the supernatural order pertaining to society are undervalued or neglected; on the contrary, it is readily acknowledged that while the supernatural supposes the natural, yet the supernatural order rises far above the natural order and supplements its many deficiencies. It is, however, because the particular approach to our present problem is from the philosophical point of view that attention is focused on the natural order.

Finally, the point of view taken in this study is specifically Thomistic. It is a Thomistic conception of international society. Consequently, in the development of the thesis the guiding norm will be the doctrine of Thomism, and the selection of source materials will be made from writers who belong to the Thomistic tradition. This again is not to overlook or deny the contributions made by others to the study of international society. Among these must be mentioned especially Francis Suarez, the famous Jesuit philosopher, theologian, and jurist, who shares with Francis de Vitoria the honor of being an outstanding Catholic pioneer in the field of international law. But Suarez was not a Thomist, as was Vitoria, and consequently his contributions, while justly deserving of acknowledgement, remain outside the scope of this work.

The writer takes this occasion to acknowledge with gratitude the opportunity afforded him by the Right Reverend Ignatius Esser, O.S.B., to pursue the course of graduate studies in Philosophy at the Catholic University of America. At the same time he wishes to express his appreciation and gratitude to his major professor and dean, the Very Reverend Doctor Ignatius Smith, O.P., for the kindness, encouragement, and assistance extended to him throughout the course of studies and in the preparation of this dissertation. Expressions of appreciation are likewise due to the Reverend Doctor Robert Slavin, O.P., and to the Reverend Doctor William McDonald, for reading the manuscript and offering helpful suggestions, as well as to the other members of the Faculty of Philosophy whose courses have been followed at the Catholic University. Grateful acknowledgement is also made to the personnel of "The Catholic Association for International Peace" and the "Carnegie Endowment for International Peace" for suggesting and providing much of the source material used in this study, as well as to the Catholic University Library and the Library of Congress for the use of their library facilities. Finally, acknowledgment is made to the publishers and authors for permission to reprint passages from their copyrighted works. If expressly requested by the publisher, specific mention of this permission is made in connection with each passage quoted. In other instances only the names of the authors and publishers are indicated, but their generous permissions are hereby likewise gratefully acknowledged.

CHAPTER I

HISTORICAL SURVEY OF ATTEMPTS AND PROPOSALS FOR INTERNATIONAL ORGANIZATION

As an introduction to the study of the philosophical principles which must form the basis of any true international or universal society, the development of the concept of such a society will be traced historically through the principal attempts and proposals for world organization which have been made in the past. The purpose of this chapter is not to attempt a complete historical treatment of the subject, but simply to indicate the outstanding features in this development as an evidence of the constant tradition and desire of mankind for some form of world unity. Consequently, the emphasis will not be on the historical influences which occasioned these various attempts or proposals for world unity, nor on the juridical and technical questions of organization, but rather on the philosophical ideas underlying them. The historical circumstances surrounding these attempts and proposals must, of course, be considered, as well as the broad outlines of the machinery of organization, but only in so far as they form the setting and concrete expression of the fundamental ideas on which they were based.

I. THE ANCIENT WORLD

A. THE WORLD EMPIRES OF THE ORIENT

In tracing the attempts at the unification of peoples and political groups in antiquity, it is preferable to characterize the relations between these groups as a form of world organization, rather than of international organization.[1] The same is true of the Middle Ages. Strictly speaking, one

[1] Lange, Christian, *Histoire de l'internationalisme, I: jusqu'à la Paix de Westphalie*, Kristiania: H. Aschehoug, 1919, p. 19.

1

can speak of an international organization or an international society only if the members of that society are independent and sovereign national states, such as arose at the close of the Middle Ages and in early modern times. The distinction, however, is chiefly one of terminology. The underlying principles in each case are fundamentally the same.

The term "world organization," as applied to the peoples of antiquity, is evidently subject to the spatial limitations of the world as it was known at that time. To the Assyrians and Persians, the world was coextensive with western Asia and the fringes of Europe and Africa adjacent to it; to the Greeks, it was confined to the narrower limits of the Hellenic race and culture; to the Romans, the world orbit was much larger, extending to practically all of Europe, western Asia, and northern Africa. So also in the Middle Ages, the world as a political community, was coextensive with "Christendom." The problem of world organization is, therefore, not one of spatial extension, but rather of a unifying principle which serves to coordinate the peoples or political communities conceived in each instance as constituting the civilized world.[2]

Although the great monarchs of western Asia, the kings of the Assyrians and the Persians, envisaged a universal or world empire in which all known peoples would be united under one rule, they were inspired, so far as we can ascertain, solely by the desire to conquer and subdue. Their guiding principle was that of personal aggrandizement, might, and power. The world empires of the East have been aptly described as "Empires of Power," in contradistinction to the later Roman Empire, which was an "Empire of Government."[3] The rulers of the Assyrian and Persian Empires, who believed it their mission to dominate all peoples, regarded these peoples, not as citizens, but solely as

[2] *Ibid.*, p. 19.
[3] du Plessis, Jean, *The Human Caravan*, New York: Sheed and Ward, 1939, p. 128.

subjects of their world State.[4] Here one looks in vain for the idea of a universal organization, the coordination of the various elements without the empire, and *a fortiori* for the idea of a community of nations or peoples forming one world unit.[5]

B.   THE GREEK FEDERATIONS

The Greeks present a different picture. When history reveals the Hellenes to us, we find them organized in independent tribes, which later developed into the city-states, the political communities of Greek antiquity, which formed the subject of the classical political treatises of Plato and Aristotle. The coexistence of these free and independent city-states encouraged interstate relationships. Since these city-states were sovereign and independent political communities, their mutual relations were not simply intermunicipal, but really, though in a restricted sense (restricted, that is, to the limited sphere of the Hellenic world), international. On this point Phillipson writes:

> The Greek municipalities being autonomous and equal before the law, they present an adequate correspondence to the modern civilized States, constituting the family of nations; and their 'intermunicipal law' offers a sufficiently valid counterpart to modern international law.[6]

Even though warfare seemed to be the normal condition of interstate relations at the beginning of Greek history, there were, nevertheless, certain common bonds which tended to unite these independent political communities into a community of states. Chief among these bonds were: a common heritage, racial at first, but cultural rather than racial in later periods; a common religion; the develop-

---

[4] Schücking, Walther, *Die Organisation der Welt*, Leipzig: Alfred Kröner, 1909, p. 11.

[5] Lange, *op. cit.*, p. 20.

[6] Phillipson, Coleman, *The International Law and Custom of Ancient Greece and Rome*, 2 vols., London: Macmillan, 1911, vol. I, p. 62. (Reprinted by permission of the Macmillan Company, publishers.)

ment of Greek moral philosophy.[7]   In the course of centuries these unifying forces developed to the extent that peace and cooperation, instead of war, came to be regarded as the normal condition of interstate relations.

> Never was the ancient world so near to surmounting the ancient belief in war as the natural condition of interstatal life as in the VI–IV Century B.C. [In Greece]. Never was it so ready to accept as normal the condition of peace between different Greek States, a theory altogether similar to our own modern concept.[8]

The existence of friendly relations and cooperation between the Greek city-states is evidenced by the numerous treaties which have come down to us through contemporary historians. But these individual and temporary agreements are not our primary concern. What evidence is there for a universal organization among the Greek city-states? While there was never a universal Hellenic society of states embracing all the city-states, historians of international relations generally refer to three examples of Greek federations which included a large number of these states. The first of these is primarily religious in origin and object, the Amphictyonic League; the other two are strictly political, the Athenian and Achean Leagues.[9]

The earliest form of Greek intertribal or intercity organization consisted of religious associations, called "amphictyonies," formed for the purpose of carrying out common religious functions and of protecting and embellishing common religious shrines. The most famous of these associations is the Delphian Amphictyonic League, composed originally of twelve independent Greek tribes. The Amphictyonic Council, the representative assembly of the League, met twice each year, in the spring at Delphi and in

---

[7] Rostovtseff, Michael I., "International Relations in the Ancient World" in Walsh, E. A., *The History and Nature of International Relations*, New York: Macmillan, 1922, p. 46.

[8] *Ibid.*, p. 46.

[9] e. g., York, Elizabeth, *League of Nations, Ancient, Mediaeval, and Modern*, London: The Swarthmore Press, 1919, chapter I.

the autumn near Thermopylae. This Council was composed of two representatives from each tribe, each having an equal vote. The object and functions of the Council, at least in the beginning, were exclusively religious, centering about the guardianship of the sacred shrines, but gradually the Council attained authority also in non-religious matters. Since religion played such an integral part in the daily life of the early Greeks, it was inevitable that it should have at least some influence on the political life of the people.

> Hence we see how various political matters were necessarily interwoven with the seemingly exclusive religious jurisdiction of the Amphictyonic Council. Beginning with the practice of pronouncing on charges as to infractions of interstatal or international rights of a sacred description, the Council gradually assumed competence in regard to divers non-religious questions, and occasionally exercised control in political matters of far reaching importance.[10]

Although the influence of the Amphictyonic League on Greek interstatal thought and practice and on later international movements might be easily overestimated, yet, on the other hand, it cannot be lightly dismissed as being of no consequence. That it did produce some tangible political results seems quite certain. It exercised a great influence, directly or indirectly, on the promotion of a common feeling of unity among the Greeks.[11] It was the first council in Europe, to our knowledge, to attempt a limitation of warfare and its cruelties; according to the ancient oath taken by members of the Amphictyonic Council, each pledged respect for the territory of the other: no member would destroy the city of another member, nor cut off its water supply, either in time of war or peace.[12] According to York, the Amphictyonic Council served as the model for prac-

[10] Phillipson, *op. cit.*, II, p. 9. (Reprinted by permission of the Macmillan Company, publishers.)

[11] *Ibid.*, II, p. 11.

[12] Stawell, F. Melian, *The Growth of International Thought*, New York: Henry Holt, 1930, p. 23.

tically all of the great European plans for world organization; hence "in the far off days of ancient Greece, we find
the original germ of the fruitful idea of a League of
Nations."[13]

More political in nature were the military and naval con-
federations or leagues of Greek city-states. Chief among
these were the Confederacy of Delos, also known as the
Athenian League because of the rôle which Athens played
as its head, and the Achaean League. The former was organized in the fifth century B.C., as a means of common defence of Hellenic cities against the threat of Persian domination. It comprised, not all the Greek cities, but chiefly
the maritime states, who pledged to contribute either ships
or money for the common fleet—"the first instance of an
international navy and police force."[14] Its juridical or-
ganition consisted of a Federal Council, which met peri-
odically in the sanctuary of Apollo at Delos; it determined
the policies of the League and exercised legal and arbitral
jurisdiction between member states as a federal tribunal.[15]
The League, however, lasted hardly more than fifty years.
Its failure was due to the defection of the allies, but principally to the aspirations of Athens—contrary to the best
political thought of the Athenian philosophers—for hegemony and subsequent sovereignty over the entire Confederation.[16]

The Achaean League, originally a small, but strong confederation in Achaia, was expanded into a Pan-Hellenic
Federation, after the death of Alexander the Great, as a
common defense measure against Macedonia and the growing power of Rome. At the height of its power, the Achaean
League comprised about seventy Greek city-states. The organization of the League was federal, consisting of an Assembly, in which each city had an equal vote, a Council,
which prepared the agenda, a Senate, about which little is
known, a Federal Court, and a Cabinet of ten members. The
League was headed by a President or General, called

---

[13] York, *op. cit.*, p. 8.   [15] Phillipson, *op. cit.*, II, p. 15.
[14] *Ibid.*, p. 25.   [16] *Ibid.*, II, p. 15.

"Strategus." Both the President and the members of the Cabinet were elected annually by the Assembly.[17] As a military measure, the Achaean League failed to achieve its primary purpose of safeguarding Greek independence, for it arose too late to check the invasion of Roman power; as a political organization, it also failed to achieve lasting unity and solidarity among the Greek states; but as a classic example of federal organization, it has survived to the present time, as is evidenced by the tribute paid to it by the men who were responsible for the framing of the Constitution of the United States.

Though attempts to bring about unity and mutual co-operation in the Greek world were not lacking, the end was never fully achieved. The failure of the Greek world to form a genuine and permanent community of states may be attributed to the following factors: a narrow racism, cultural rather than biological, which tended to exclude all those considered inferior by birth or culture; an exaggerated patriotism or nationalism, which identified the citizen too closely with his own city-state; jealousy and rivalry between city-states for hegemony and ultimate supremacy.[18]

C. GREEK COSMOPOLITANISM

While the Greek cities were organizing federations for their common defence against the outside world, certain Greek philosophers, transcending the confines of the Hellenic world, were developing the concept of universal human solidarity, which must necessarily form the foundation of a genuine world society. Socrates is regarded as the first to proclaim himself a "citizen of the world"; although he was loyal to the laws of his own city-state, even to the point of death, yet this did not exclude him from citizenship in the universal community of mankind.[19] The Cynics also proclaimed themselves to be citizens of the world, but their

[17] York, *op. cit.*, p. 31.
[18] Phillipson, *op. cit.*, I, p. 63.
[19] Schücking, *op. cit.*, p. 11.

cosmopolitanism was negative, rather than positive. It was a reaction against the narrow racism and nationalism of the Greek city-states as well as the "natural institution" of slavery.[20] It remained for the Stoics to give a positive content to this negative cosmopolitanism: in the world-state of Zeno, all mankind would form one great community and lead a life of unity and order. Plutarch thus sums up the teaching of Zeno in his treatise "On the Fortune or the Virtue of Alexander."

> The much-admired *Republic* of Zeno, the founder of the Stoic sect, may be summed up in this one main principle: that all the inhabitants of this world of ours should not live differentiated by their respective rules of justice into separate cities and communities, but that we should consider all men to be of one community and one polity, and that we should have a common life and an order common to us all, even as a herd that feeds together and shares the pasturage of a common field. This Zeno wrote, giving shape to a dream or, as it were, shadowy picture of a well-ordered and philosophic commonwealth. . . .[21]

The World Empire of Alexander the Great was to a great extent the external expression of the contemporary philosophy of cosmopolitanism, even though it antedated the full development of that philosophy. Although Alexander was the pupil of Aristotle, his idea of the perfect political community was not the city-state. He had visions of a universal empire. To the aspirations of the Assyrian and Persian monarchs for world supremacy, however, Alexander joined the philosophy of cosmopolitanism and the concept of the Greek city-state as the center and source of culture. The object of his conquest was not so much world domination as the extension of a common civilization and culture

---

[20] *Ibid.*, p. 12.

[21] Plutarch, "On the Fortune or the Virtue of Alexander," § 6, *Moralia*, vol. IV (Loeb Classical Library), Cambridge: Harvard University Press, 1936. (Reprinted by permission of the President and Fellows of Harvard College.)

to the entire known world.[22] But Alexander's Empire was too short-lived to achieve any permanent results.

D. THE ROMAN EMPIRE

What Alexander envisaged, but failed to achieve, remained for the Romans to accomplish. Two elements in the formation of the Roman Empire may be distinguished: a material and a formal element. Its material element is the vast complexus of territories and peoples which composed the Roman Empire at the height of its power. In the beginning of its era of conquest and expansion, Rome was undoubtedly motivated to a very great extent by the same principle which inspired the ancient oriental monarchs, namely, the desire to dominate and rule as mistress of the world.[23] But this was not the only motive. Economic reasons were also present: the necessity of providing for their own existence required the Romans to seek for supplies outside of their limited territory. And since the ancient world had not as yet familiarized itself with the coexistence of rival powers living in mutual cooperation, its solution of the problem of self-preservation lay in the absorption of other peoples and their territories into the realm of the more powerful.[24]

But there was another element active in this vast project, which may be designated as a formal element in that it gave a certain homogeneous form to the otherwise heterogeneous collection of lands and peoples gathered under one rule by the might of the Roman military dictatorship. This element is complex, rather than simple; a combination of factors, rather than one single principle, accounts for the final uni-

[22] "It was Alexander who gave effect to the idea [of Zeno]. For Alexander did not follow Aristotle's advice to treat the Greeks as if he were their leader, and other peoples as if he were their master. . . . But, as he believed that he came as a heaven-sent governor to all, and as a mediator for the whole world . . . he bade them all consider as their fatherland the whole inhabited earth."—*Ibid.*, § 6.

[23] Schücking, *op. cit.*, p. 15.

[24] Lange, *op. cit.*, pp. 20-21.

fication of all the peoples subjected to Roman arms into a universal society or community of nations. Of these factors, three may be singled out for consideration: the Roman concept and genius for law and organization, the cultural heritage derived from the Greeks, and the philosophy of cosmopolitanism. It is at once evident that these factors were not isolated threads, but were closely interwoven in the production of the Roman universal society.

It was its concept of law and its genius for legal organization which distinguished Rome's "Empire of Government" from the oriental "Empires of Power." Law has always been associated with the name of Rome. From the earliest days of the Republic, the lives of the citizens of Rome were regulated by the *jus civile*, those of foreigners living in the City by the *jus gentium*, which, according to the commonly accepted opinion, originally consisted of the basic principles which were common to the laws of the various peoples in contact with Rome.[25] This system of law, which was destined to become the law of the world, owes its particular principles and usages to the Roman magistrates and jurists, but is indebted to the Greeks for its philosophical basis. As McIlwain states it:

> The philosophical basis of Roman law is Greek, and it was laid in the Republican period, but the particular principles of the law itself are Roman, worked out step by step with patient thoroughness by generations of magistrates and jurists.[26]

It was the combination of these two elements which, according to Scott, produced the universal law of the ancient civilized world, coextensive with the Roman Empire, and laid the foundations for later international law. Scott accounts for this development by a two-fold identification:

[25] Scott, James Brown, *Law, the State, and the International Community*, 2 vols., New York: Columbia University Press, 1939, vol. I, p. 111.

[26] McIlwain, Charles H., *The Growth of Political Thought in the West*, New York: Macmillan, 1932, p. 121. (Reprinted by permission of the Macmillan Company, publishers.)

> There are two identifications which have greatly affected Roman Law and therefore its contribution to jurisprudence. The first identification, that of the *ius gentium* with the Roman civil law, resulted in the universal law of the ancient civilized world; the second identification, that of the *ius gentium* with the conception of natural law derived from the Greeks, and especially from the Stoics, eventually resulted in the formation of an international law.[27]

With the gradual extension of the civil law of Rome and the rights of citizenship to all free men within the Empire, which reached its culmination in the third century after Christ, a genuine world organization, based on a universal law, was brought into being. Though the materials for this vast organization were acquired by military power, it was the Roman law and its reliance on the moral force of justice rather than on the physical force of arms, which put order and unity into this organization, and made it an "Empire of Government," rather than an "Empire of Power." Hill, in his *History of Diplomacy*, thus describes the reign of the universal Roman law:

> When Caracalla, in 212, extended to all free men throughout the Empire the full rights of Roman citizenship, there was but one law for the whole western world,—the Civil Law of Rome. A form of government had been brought into existence which embraced in its conception the whole of humanity and embodied the wide diversity of its races and the still greater variety of its usages in a vast world state. Never before in the history of mankind had a rule so universal been established.[28]

The second factor contributing to the unification of peoples within the Roman Empire was the cultural heritage which Rome derived from the Greeks. Within the Hellenic

[27] Scott, James Brown, *Law, the State, and the International Community*, vol. I, p. 107. (Reprinted by permission of the Columbia University Press.)

[28] Hill, D. J., *History of Diplomacy in the International Development of Europe*, 3 vols., New York: Longmans, Green, 1905, vol. I, pp. 13-14.

world, as has already been seen, no complete and permanent political unity had been achieved, but there was a definite cultural and intellectual unity. The Greeks had attained a culture universal in application and superior to anything which the world had known up to that time. From the very beginnings of Roman expansion, the culture of the Greeks was present as an active leaven, and from this process developed the Graeco-Roman civilization which became the civilization of the world under the Empire. Dawson clearly states the effects of this developmental process:

> The result of this process, no doubt, represents a victory for the Roman sword and the Roman genius for organization, but socially and intellectually it was the Greeks who conquered. The age of Romanisation of the Hellenic East was also the age of the Hellenisation of the Roman West, and the two movements converged to form a cosmopolitan civilization, unified by the Roman political and military organisation, but based on the Hellenistic tradition of culture and inspired by Greek social ideals.[29]

Closely associated with the cultural heritage of the Greeks, or rather a part of it, was the philosophical concept of mankind as a single world society, the cosmopolitanism of Zeno and the Stoics. As we have already seen, the principal tenet of Zeno, as related by Plutarch, was that all men should be considered as forming one universal social and political community. The influence of Zeno on Roman political thought is unmistakable, and may be clearly seen in the writings of some of Rome's greatest thinkers and statesmen. Cicero is perhaps the greatest Roman political philosopher and statesman to give evidence of this influence. Several passages are sufficient to indicate this.

> ... the unanimity of the races of the world must be regarded as a law of nature.[30]

[29] Dawson, Christopher, *The Making of Europe*, New York: Sheed and Ward, 1938, p. 5.

[30] Cicero, Marcus Tullius, *Tusculan Disputations*, I, xiii, 30. (Loeb Classical Library), New York: Putnam's, 1917. (This and succeeding

... it is our duty to respect, defend, and maintain
the common bonds of union and fellowship sub-
sisting between all the members of the human
race.[31]

But in the whole moral sphere of which we are
speaking there is nothing more glorious nor of
wider range than the solidarity of mankind, that
species of alliance and partnership of interests and
that actual affection which exists between man and
man.[32]

Seneca expressly describes the society of mankind as a
commonwealth and gives it priority in dignity over the local
commonwealth:

Let us grasp the idea that there are two common-
wealths—the one, a vast and truly common state,
which embraces alike gods and men, in which we
look neither to this corner of earth nor to that, but
measure the bounds of our citizenship by the path
of the sun; the other, the one to which we have
been assigned by the accident of birth.[33]

The philosophical conception of cosmopolitanism reached
its apogee in the person of the Philosopher-Emperor, Marcus Aurelius Antonius. To him every man was a citizen of
the Universe, "the highest state, of which all other states
are but as households."[34] The common bond which unites all
men as citizens of the Universe is reason and the natural
law:

If the intellectual capacity is common to us all,
common too is the reason, which makes us rational
creatures. If so, that reason also is common which

quotations from Loeb Classical Library are reprinted by permission
of the President and Fellows of Harvard College.)

[31] Cicero, Marcus Tullius, *De officiis*, I, xli, 149. (Loeb Classical
Library), New York: Macmillan, 1913.

[32] Cicero, Marcus Tullius, *De finibus*, V, xxiii, 65 (Loeb Classical
Library), New York: Macmillan, 1914.

[33] Seneca, Lucius Annaeus, *De otio*, IV, 1, in *Moral Essays*, vol. II
(Loeb Classical Library), New York: Putnam's, 1928.

[34] Marcus Aurelius Antoninus, *The Communings with Himself of
Marcus Aurelius Antoninus*, III, 11 (Loeb Classical Library), New
York: Putnam's, 1916.

tells us to do or not to do. If so, law also is common. If so, we are citizens. If so, we are fellow-members of an organized community. If so, the Universe is as it were a state—for of what other single polity can the whole race of mankind be said to be fellow-members?[35]

That these philosophical concepts had a genuine influence on Roman governmental organization and policy is quite certain; no clearer evidence could be found than the constant and progressive extension of the rights of Roman citizenship, and consequently of Roman law, during the era of the Republic, and especially under the Empire. In the first stages of its career of conquest, Rome jealously reserved the privileges of citizenship to its own nationals; all others were subjects and foreigners. But the extension of Roman ctizenship to non-Romans, first to the peoples of Italy, than to province after province outside of Italy, began under the Republic, was accelerated during the imperial era, and reached its culmination when the Emperor Caracalla in 212 A.D. granted the privileges of citizenship to all free men living within the confines of the Empire. Thus the Roman State was officially declared to be coextensive with the civilized world, and within this World-State the community of mankind was recognized as a fact and given legal status, fulfilling in some measure Zeno's dream of a well-ordered and philosophic universal commonwealth.[36]

To describe the Roman Empire as the ideal universal society of mankind would, of course, be utterly misleading. It would be necessary to advert only to two such hideous blotches on this society as the universal institution of slavery and the inhuman persecutions of the Christians to dispel any illusions of this kind. But that the Roman Empire did bring numerous benefits to the millions of people living within its orbit cannot be gainsaid. Among these were the common and universal law which promoted justice and internal peace, which, in turn, contributed greatly to the development of commerce and material prosperity, of

---

[35] *Ibid.*, IV, 4.   [36] Schücking, *op. cit.*, p. 15.

culture and the arts. As regards the cherished *Pax Romana,* Hill writes:

> Perhaps the crowning benefit conferred by the Roman Empire upon its vast population was the 'Roman peace.' Within the imperial limits there was little disposition to revolt, for the advantages of just laws, unrestrained intercourse, and a uniform administration were highly prized. Classes continued to exist, but the ancient national and racial prejudices and antagonisms largely disappeared.[37]

Perhaps no one has left us a more glowing account of the beneficial effects of the Empire's universal rule than the Christian poet Prudentius who wrote shortly before the dissolution of that Empire. As a Christian, Prudentius regarded the Roman Empire as the design of God to unite mankind in preparation for the coming of Christ and the propagation of the Faith.

> What is the secret of Rome's historical destiny? It is that God wills the unity of mankind, since the religion of Christ demands a social foundation of peace and international amity. Hitherto the whole earth from east to west had been rent asunder by continual strife. To curb this madness God has taught the nations to be obedient to the same laws and all to become Romans. Now we see mankind living as citizens of one city and members of a common household. Men come from distant lands across the seas to one common forum, and the peoples are united by commerce and culture and intermarriage. From the intermingling of peoples a single race is born. This is the meaning of all the victories and triumphs of the Roman Empire: the Roman peace has prepared the road for the coming of Christ.[38]

Although the Roman Empire was a universal organization, it was not an international society in the strict sense of

---

[37] Hill, *op. cit.,* I, p. 15.

[38] Prudentius, *Contra Symmachum,* II, 578-636. Migne, *Patres Latini,* Vol. 60, Col. 226-230. English translation from Dawson, *op. cit.,* p. 23.

the term as we now use it to mean a society of states. Politically, the Empire was composed of subordinate provinces, not coordinate and autonomous states; it was a single world-state, rather than a society of states. Culturally, it tended to destroy originality in the various racial groups by the substitution and establishment of a uniform Greco-Roman civilization, at least for the upper classes.[39] Yet, despite these defects, the achievements of the Roman Empire toward the unification of mankind are without parallel in history. Long after the dissolution of the Empire through internal decay, the infiltration of barbaric elements, and the rupture between East and West, the Empire continued to exist in the minds of men as the symbol of human unity and as the exemplar of universal political organization. It influenced the great political thinkers of the Middle Ages and after; it remained the political ideal for European imperial rulers from Charlemagne to Napoleon.[40]

II.   THE MIDDLE AGES

A.   CHRISTENDOM—THE SYMBOL AND FACT OF MEDIAEVAL UNITY

To many people the very notion of mediaeval unity is paradoxical; their picture of mediaeval Europe is that of an heterogeneous aggregation of petty feudal kingdoms and principalities whose chief occupation consisted in making war upon one another. But such a view is, needless to say, very defective and misleading; at most it represents only one phase of mediaeval Europe, and even then looks only upon the surface of things, missing entirely the unifying principles that lay beneath the surface. It is true that after the dissolution of the Roman Empire in the West, Europe was divided into a number of tribal kingdoms, which under the feudal system were further partitioned into innumerable small quasi-independent feudal states, and which towards the close of the Middle Ages were again consolidated along

---

[39] Lange, *op. cit.*, p. 21.   [40] *Ibid.*, p. 22.

regional and racial lines to form the modern national states. This is but one side of the picture. On the other hand, there were periods of mediaeval history when Western Europe presented a genuine external political unity in the form of the Carolingian Empire and the Teutonic Holy Roman Empire. But even apart from this external political unity, mediaeval Europe, despite its multiplicity of kingdoms and principalities, was characterized by a genuine unity, implicit if not always explicit, which was deeply rooted in the religion and culture of the people. Two important factors contributed to this unity: the memory and influence of the Roman Empire, with its universal rule and culture, and, by far the more important factor, Christianity.

To the mediaeval mind, the ancient Roman Empire was a cherished memory, a symbol, and an ideal. But it was more than a dream or a figment of the imagination; it was a real force, not merely potential, but actual, in the formation of a unified civilization in mediaeval Western Europe. Chief among the legacies inherited from ancient Rome were the concept of a common law and a single rule, the desire for universal peace and order, a common language, and a common culture. The new racial elements from Northern and Eastern Europe gradually assimilated the Roman ideals and culture, which, joined to their own contributions, became the common culture of the Middle Ages. Christopher Dawson thus sums up the influence of Rome on mediaeval Europe:

> The new Christian Rome ... was indeed destined to inherit the Roman tradition and to preserve the old ideal of Roman unity in a changed world. For it was to Rome that the new peoples owed the very idea of the possibility of a common civilization. Through all the chaos of the dark ages that were to follow, men cherished the memory of the universal peace and order of the Roman Empire, with its common religion, its common law and its common culture; and the repeated efforts of the Middle Ages to return to the past and to recover this lost unity and civilization led the new peoples forward

to the future and prepared the way for the coming of a new European culture.[41]

But the most powerful force making for unity in mediaeval Europe was Christianity. For centuries, Western Europe, conterminous with Latin Christianity, was designated by a single name: Christendom, *Respublica Christiana,* or *Imperium Christianum.* Christendom was not simply a theoretical ideal, but a sociological fact. As Jarret points out, "it is necessary to remember that Christendom to the men of that time [Middle Ages] was a single and living organism, and that Christendom was conterminous with the Catholic Faith."[42]

Christianity as a religion is itself a unifying force, for it contains fundamental doctrines which make for unity among its adherents: the oneness of God, the Creator and Ruler of the universe, the common origin and destiny of mankind in God, the essential equality of man, irrespective of race or social condition, the Redemption of all mankind through Jesus Christ, the solidarity of all Christians forming the Mystical Body of Christ, the true brotherhood of man under the Fatherhood of God. It was precisely because these fundamental doctrines were not simply theoretical truths, but were recognized as an actual fact, that mediaeval Christendom was a "single and living organism." The influence of these doctrines on mediaeval political unity has been aptly expressed by Bryce:

> It is on the religious life that nations repose. Because divinity was divided, humanity had been divided likewise; the doctrine of the unity of God now enforced the unity of man, who had been created in His image. The first lesson of Christianity was love, a love that was to join in one body those whom suspicion and pride of race had hitherto kept apart. There was thus formed by the new

[41] Dawson, *op. cit.,* pp. 23-24.
[42] Jarrett, Bede, *Social Theories of the Middle Ages,* Boston: Little, Brown and Co., 1926, p. 213.

religion a community of the faithful, a Holy Empire designed to gather all men into its bosom. . . .[43]

According to Carlton Hayes, it was Christendom, rather than the Holy Roman Empire, which was the concrete expression of the mediaeval desire for unity and universality:

> Just when the Roman Empire was disintegrating and when feudalism was developing with its localism and private warfare, the persistent longing for universality found fruitful expression, not so much in the Byzantine Empire or in a Holy Roman Empire of the German Nation, as in the concept of Christendom. And Christendom was a fact, not a theory.[44]

As a corollary to the influence of the doctrines of Christianity on mediaeval unity, mention must be made of the intellectual development, especially in the field of philosophy, which reached its climax in the thirteenth century. The University of Paris became the intellectual center of Europe, truly cosmopolitan in its faculty and student body, whence was diffused throughout all Christendom the philosophical synthesis achieved by the Scholastics, and particularly by St. Thomas Aquinas. In his brochure, *Die Organisation der Welt*, Schücking shows how the principle of unity, inspired by the notion of God as the one Infinite Being, permeated the whole of mediaeval thought, even in its social and political aspects.[45]

[43] Bryce, James, *The Holy Roman Empire*, New York: A. L. Burt, 1886, p. 89.

[44] Hayes, Carlton J. H., "Mediaeval Diplomacy" in Walsh, *op. cit.*, p. 73.

[45] "Zwar begegnen wir der Weltreichsidee im ganzen Mittelalter, sie wird getragen nicht nur von der Erinnerung der Antike und den Grundlehren des Christentums, sondern auch von der mittelalterlichen philosophischen Anschauung mit ihrem principium unitatis. Gott ist das einheitliche Sein, das einheitliche Sein Gottes aber durchdringt das Weltganze, so dass auch hier wieder das Prinzip der Einheit herrschen muss." Schücking, *op. cit.*, p. 22.

B. THE MEDIAEVAL EMPIRE

The principle of unity inherent in Christendom received external political expression in the universal Christian Empire of the Middle Ages. Although mediaeval Western Europe was never organized under the single all-powerful and all-embracing rule as was the Roman world under the ancient Empire, yet it was sufficiently united during two distinct periods so as to be properly designated as a universal Christian Empire, briefly under Charlemagne in the ninth century, and later under Otto and his successors. The Empire of Western Europe, or Christendom, was conceived throughout the Middle Ages, not as a new creation, but as the logical and actual continuation of the ancient Roman Empire, as is apparent from its designation as the "Holy Roman Empire," or simply as the "Roman Empire."

The Roman Empire, which had continued to exist in theory in the East under the Byzantine Emperors, was revived in the West by the coronation of Charlemagne by Pope Leo III at St. Peter's in Rome on Christmas Day in the year 800 A.D. This imperial coronation was not an empty gesture or a mere symbol. By inheritance and conquest Charlemagne had succeeded in bringing under his control practically all of Western Europe. Consequently, it was to this powerful Frankish chief that the Pope in Rome looked for protection, rather than to the powerless emperor in Byzantium. It was regarded as the opportune and providential moment for the restoration of the Roman Empire in the West, the tradition of which had always been kept alive by the Papacy.[46]

But the Empire of Charlemagne was extremely short-lived. It was the achievement of a single dominating personality which scarcely survived its founder; it lacked the solid basis of a well developed culture and political organization. As Dawson observes, "the germs of decay were inherent in the Carolingian State from its origin."[47] It was not merely to the attacks from without or to the Frankish

[46] Schücking, *op. cit.*, p. 18.   [47] Dawson, *op. cit.*, p. 256.

custom of dividing a realm among all the sons of the king that the dissolution of the Carolingian Empire was entirely due, for the Empire contained within itself from the very beginning the contradictory principles of Roman and Christian universalism on the one hand and Germanic particularism on the other.

> It [the Carolingian Empire] claimed to be the Roman Empire, but it was in fact the Frankish monarchy, and so it embodied two contradictory principles, the universalism of the Roman and Christian traditions on the one hand, and the tribal particularism of barbaric Europe on the other.[48]

But even if the Carolingian Empire did contain the germs of decay from the start, it also embodied, as Dawson likewise observes, the ideal of unity which was destined to attain fuller development in the centuries to come.

> And yet it was also the embodiment and representative of an ideal, and this ideal, in spite of its apparent failure, proved more durable and persistent than any of the military or political achievements of the period. It outlived the state to which it had given birth and survived through the anarchy that followed, to become the principle of the new order which arose in the West and in the eleventh century.[49]

The new order was the revival of the Roman Empire, after a century of disintegration, under the leadership of the Saxons. In 962 Otto I, King of the Saxons, went to Rome and received the imperial crown from Pope John XII, which event marks the beginning of the Holy Roman Empire. Like that of Charlemagne, Otto's Empire was regarded by the people of the time as the continuation of the ancient Roman Empire in the West. While the Holy Roman Empire never achieved a universality of rule and power comparable with that of the ancient Roman Empire, it was nevertheless destined to exercise considerable influence on the course of European history for several centuries. In territorial extent the Holy Roman Empire never equalled

[48] *Ibid.*, p. 256. [49] *Ibid.*, p. 257.

even the Empire of Charlemagne, yet it did possess a more durable political organization. It is the opinion of Schücking that the secret of this durability lay in the appreciation of the Germanic concept of tribal patriotism and tribal hierarchical organization, and the conjunction of this principle of the hierarchical organization of subordinate groups with the principle of a unified rule inherited from the ancient Roman and the Carolingian Empire. Charlemagne had failed to recognize the existence of relatively autonomous tribal groups as one of the essential features of Germanic political theory, and the dissolution of his Empire was the reaction of the Germanic peoples to the imposition of the ancient Roman concept of uniformity. The Empire of Otto was built upon the Germanic principle of hierarchical subordination: within the Empire, individual territories could remain intact and retain their own individual rulers, subject, however, to the Emperor.[50]

Although the Holy Roman Empire survived as an active power in Western Europe for several centuries, it never fully succeeded in achieving political unity and harmony among all the peoples of Christendom. Its sphere of influence was limited chiefly to Germany and Italy. And even within that limited sphere its history is marred by continuous contests and struggles, especially with the Papacy. In theory, the relations between the Empire and the Papacy, made explicit by Pope St. Gelasius in the fifth century, were clear enough: within Christendom, or the Church of God, there are two powers; the one spiritual, vested in the Pope, which pertains to all matters concerning man's eternal salvation; the other temporal, held by the Emperor, which concerns the regulation of matters pertaining to man's temporal well-being. But in practice the two powers did not always work in harmony in the manner in which Pope St. Gelasius had described them. From the very beginning, the Holy Roman Emperors sought to enhance their own authority at the expense of the Pope by usurping powers

[50] Schücking, *op. cit.*, p. 19.

distinctly spiritual in nature, such as the appointment and investing of bishops, and even the selection of their own candidates for the Papacy. On the other hand, it must also be admitted that the Popes were often involved in disputes for temporal possessions which brought them into conflict with the Emperors. But it was chiefly because of their own personal ambitions that the Emperors as a whole failed to realize their special task and mission as the protector and leader of Christendom, as the bond of unity among Christian peoples, as the *pacificator mundi.*[51]

Yet, in spite of all its shortcomings, the Holy Roman Empire bears eloquent testimony to the ideal of unity that was never absent in the Middle Ages, a unity primarily religious in nature which permeated the Christian social, cultural, and political world.

C.   THE PAPACY AS A FACTOR IN MEDIAEVAL UNITY

Without doubt, the most important single institution in the Middle Ages was the Catholic Church. Mention has already been made of the fundamental doctrines of the Church which promote unity among its members. But even a brief survey of the efforts of the Middle Ages towards the realization of political unity would be impossible without considering the important contribution of the Church as an organized spiritual society. During the Middle Ages all Christians of Western Europe recognized the spiritual authority of the Church and its visible head, the Vicar of Christ, the Pope, and looked to him for guidance. It was to the Papacy, not as a temporal power, but as the unique and divinely established spiritual power that was due its great influence in the Middle Ages. It was the Pope whom all the Christians of Western Europe, ruler and subject alike, recognized as the Head of the Church, and the Pope in his turn through the bishops of the various countries legislated, guided, and governed (spiritually) all peoples

[51] Walker, Thomas A., *A History of the Law of Nations*, 2 vols., Cambridge: At the University Press, 1899, vol. I, p. 90.

alike. It is in this unique power of the Papacy that Carlton Hayes finds the source of true mediaeval internationalism.

> It was the Papacy which, therefore, at one and the same time, by treating each nation as a separate unit, expressed in a primate with his suffragan bishops, and yet by legislating identically in matters of faith and morals for all the nations, expounded a two-fold thesis of nationalism and internationalism. The Catholic Church was by all odds the most important distinctive institution of the Middle Ages, and the Catholic Church never ceased to insist that the nations were separate individuals, yet members of a Christian brotherhood, that they were moral persons yet subject to the common law of Christendom.[52]

But apart from the general organization of the Church as a factor in promoting unity and harmony among all peoples recognizing its authority, mention must be made of certain distinct movements and efforts which had a more direct bearing on mediaeval political unity. We have already seen that it was the Papacy which kept alive the tradition of the Roman Empire in the West. It was Pope Leo III who took the initiative in the first revival of the Empire under Charlemagne. So too it was the Church, and specifically the Papacy, which took the initiative in the promotion of peace and arbitration between warring rulers.

During the age of feudalism Europe was the scene of continuous warfare, not in the modern sense of enormous military campaigns, but almost ceaseless marauding and pillaging by feudal barons and their knights. To curtail this feudal warfare there arose in France two distinct peace movements, known as the "Peace of God" and the "Truce of God." The former, originating in the tenth century, was designed to limit the scope of warfare to combatants only, thus protecting defenseless non-combatants. The latter, which arose in the next century, aimed at the limitation of warfare to certain periods of the year and certain days

[52] Hayes, "Medieval Diplomacy" in Walsh, *op. cit.*, p. 73.

of the week. These peace movements were encouraged by the Popes and received universal sanction in the Second Lateran Council in 1139.[53] In connection with the peace movements, the effect of the Crusades on the promotion of peace and unity among the peoples of Western Europe should not be overlooked. Whatever judgment may be passed upon the Crusades, it must at least be admitted that they did serve to divert the attention of rulers from domestic warfare in Europe to their common enemy in the East. Peace at home was always regarded as a necessary preliminary to the undertaking of a common expedition abroad. An example of this is the appeal of Pope Urban III at the Council of Clermont for the Crusade, in which he urged first the keeping of the peace among Christian rulers before taking any steps to organize an expedition against the Infidel.[54]

A further service rendered by the Papacy in the interest of mediaeval unity was that of arbitration. Because of its unique position as Head of the Church, to which all Christian peoples and rulers were subject alike, the Papacy was the logical tribunal for the settlement of differences between Christian States. Not that all, or even most, of these differences were submitted to the Pope for settlement; but that the Papacy was recognized as an international tribunal is evident from the number of cases on record in which disputes between Christian rulers were arbitrated by the Popes, either at the invitation of the disputants or by the injunction of the Popes themselves.[55]

III. PROPOSALS FOR INTERNATIONAL ORGANIZATION FROM THE CLOSE OF THE MIDDLE AGES UNTIL MODERN TIMES

The closing centuries of the Middle Ages witnessed the gradual development of a new political order in Europe:

[53] Robinson, Pascal, "Peace Laws and Institutions of the Mediaeval Church," *Ecclesiastical Review*, vol. LII, May 1915, pp. 527-533.

[54] *Ibid.*, p. 532.

[55] cf. Wright, R. F., *Medieval Internationalism*, London: Williams and Norgate, 1930, pp. 83-92.

the rise of the modern national states. The influence of the
Holy Roman Empire, which reached the height of its power
under the Hohenstaufens, began to wane with the fall of
that dynasty. Frederick II, the last of the Hohenstaufens,
(died 1250) was also the last of the Emperors to exert a
real influence in Italy. Thereafter the sphere of influence
of the Holy Roman Empire was limited chiefly to Germany
and the provinces to the east of Germany. On the other
hand, by the beginning of the fourteenth century the feudal
system, which distributed political power among numerous
minor nobles and prevented the concentration of authority
in the hands of strong central rulers, had been broken.
Small vassal states within the same region or country and
belonging to the same racial group were being consolidated
into larger national states. The rulers of these states, the
kings, attained power and influence to rival even that of the
Emperor. Such a king, for example, was Philip the Fair,
who ruled France from 1285 to 1314.

It will not be necessary to discuss here the various factors
which contributed to the rise of the national states. What
is important, however, is to note that the growth of these
national states, which appealed strongly to national feeling
and national glory, intensified the problem of maintaining
peace and harmony between the various peoples of Europe
and their rulers. History reveals the ever growing struggles between these states in their formative stages, each
eager for more extensive territory, greater power and
prestige, at the expense of the other. And yet these constant struggles only served to accentuate the longing of
mankind for peace, harmony, and unity among peoples. Consequently, during the centuries that follow we find numerous
proposals of high-minded and far-seeing men for the assurance of peace and unity among the nations of Europe
and of the world. In his valuable treatise on international
organization, *Der Gedanke der Internationalen Organisation
in seiner Entwicklung*, the eminent Dutch jurist, Dr. Jacob
Ter Meulen, records and discusses twenty-nine different

plans for international organization written or proposed between the years 1300 and 1800.[56]

Proposals for universal organization fall under two main heads: one is a universal rule or empire, in which all peoples recognize a single sovereign ruler, an emperor; the other is an international organization in the strict sense of the term, in which independent and sovereign states are united in some form of league or confederation, for the purpose of promoting peace and mutual cooperation. The plans cited by Meulen are all of the latter type. The greatest exponent of the former, the empire, is Dante Alighieri.

A. DANTE AND WORLD EMPIRE

It was a turbulent period and a restless country in which Dante lived—Italy at the end of the thirteenth and the beginning of the fourteenth century. After the death of Frederick II the controlling hand of the Empire had been completely withdrawn from Italy. The country was rent by factions. Confusion was increased still more by an interregnum in the Empire; no Emperor had come to Italy for fifty-eight years. Then Henry VII of Luxemburg was elected Emperor and came to Rome to be crowned in 1312. His arrival was hailed by many as an assurance of peace for a distracted country, but instead of peace he brought war. Nevertheless, it is likely that the coming of Emperor Henry VII to Italy furnished the occasion for the greatest apology for a universal empire, specifically the Holy Roman Empire,

[56] Meulen, Jacob Ter, *Der Gedanke der Internationalen Organisation in seiner Entwicklung*, I: 1300-1800, Haag: Martinus Nijhoff, 1917.

The proposals considered by Meulen are those of Pierre Dubois, King George Podiebrad of Bohemia, Erasmus, Pope Leo X, François de la Noue, Émeric Crucé, Grotius, Henry IV of France, Rachel, William Penn, John Bellers, Saint Pierre, Cardinal Alberoni, Toze, Von Loen, Saintard, Ange Goudar, Johann Franz von Palthen, Rousseau, De la Harpe and Guillard, Von Lilienfeld, an anonymous proposal for a "Holy Alliance" in 1872, Karl Gottlob Günther, a Peace Project of 1787, Jeremy Bentham, Schindler, Palier de Saint-Germain, Schlettwein, and Kant.

ever written. This was accomplished by Dante in his Latin prose work, *De Monarchia*.

De Monarchia consists of three books, the titles of which clearly indicate the contents of each: 1. "Whether Temporal Monarchy is necessary for the well-being of the world;" 2. "Whether the Roman People rightfully appropriated the office of Monarchy;" 3. "Whether the authority of the Roman Monarch derives from God immediately or from some vicar of God."[57] The second and third books, as will be noticed at once, bear the stamp of political controversies of the times, and need not detain us. It is in the first book that Dante evolves his theory, based principally on philosophical and theological grounds, for the necessity of a single world rule for all peoples, if mankind is to enjoy the peace that all desire.

In order that men may attain their end, individually, and collectively as a race, it is necessary that there be universal peace. "Whence it is necessary that universal peace is the best of those things which are ordained to our beatitude."[58]

To secure peace, government is required among men; to attain universal peace for all mankind, it is necessary that there be but one single rule for all peoples, which Dante calls a Monarchy or Empire. This is Dante's thesis. Monarchy or Empire is defined by Dante as follows: "Temporal Monarchy, called also Empire, we define as a single Principality (*unicus principatus*) extending over all peoples in time, or in those things and over those things which are measured by time."[59]

To prove his thesis on the necessity of a single world rule and a single world ruler, Dante summons an array of arguments, philosophical, theological, and poetical, which may be summarized as follows.

[57] Dante Alighieri, *De Monarchia*, translated by Aurelia Henry, Boston: Houghton Mifflin, 1904. (All quotations are cited from this edition, by permission of the Translator.)

[58] Dante, *De Monarchia*, B. I, c. 4.

[59] *Ibid.*, B. I, c. 2.

1.   When many things are ordained to the same end, one must rule and the others be ruled.   This principle applies to the individual's control of his own faculties, to the family, the village, the city, the kingdom, and by extension to the whole human race.

> We are now agreed that the whole human race is ordered for one end, as already shown.   It is meet, therefore, that the leader and lord be one, and that he be called Monarch, or Emperor.   Thus it becomes obvious that for the well-being of the world there is needed a Monarchy, or Empire.[60]

2.   "As part is related to the whole, so is the partial order related to the total order."   Individual kingdoms are only parts of the total world order.

> And so all parts which we have designated as included in kingdoms, and kingdoms themselves, should be ordered with reference to one Prince or Principality, that is, to one Monarch or Monarchy.[61]

3.   Since men are made to the image of God, they should all be one, as God is one.

> The human race, therefore, is ordered well, nay is ordered for the best, when according to the utmost of its power it becomes like unto God.   But the human race is most like unto God when it is most one, for the principle of unity dwells in Him alone. . . . But the human race is most one when all are united together, a state which is manifestly impossible unless humanity as a whole becomes subject to one Prince. . . ."[62]

4.   As all the movements of the universe are controlled by a single Divine Ruler, so should all human movements be controlled by a single human ruler.   Hence, "the human race is best ordered when in all its movements and motors it is controlled by one Prince as by one mover, by one law as by one motion."[63]

---

[60] *Ibid.*, B. I, c. 5.
[61] *Ibid.*, B. I, c. 6.
[62] *Ibid.*, B. I, c. 8.
[63] *Ibid.*, B. I, c. 9.

5.   For the settlement of disputes between princes owing no allegiance to one another, a third prince with ample jurisdiction is required to act in the capacity of judge. For the proper fulfillment of this function a single world Monarch is necessary.[64]

6.   The satisfactory administration of justice for all peoples requires the supervision of a single world Monarch. In the development of this argument, Dante is more poetical than practical; he seems to take for granted that every Emperor must necessarily be supremely just and impartial. A few sample statements will suffice.

> When cupidity is removed altogether, nothing remains inimical to Justice.... Cupidity is impossible when there is nothing to be desired, for passions cease to exist with the destruction of their objects. Since his jurisdiction is bounded only by the ocean, there is nothing for a Monarch to desire.... Who doubts now that a Monarch is most powerfully equipped for the exercise of Justice? None save he who understands not the significance of the word, for a Monarch can have no enemies.[65]

However, as Eppstein observes in connection with this argument, if Monarch is understood here in the wider sense of an international or world authority, Dante's argument is not so fantastic as it appears at first sight, for genuine international organizations do show a real concern for all men without distinction of nationality, whilst this is not always the case with state governments.[66]

7.   Mankind is happiest when most free. Mankind attains the highest freedom under a single Monarch, under whom it is best ordered, for the Monarch rules the human race for its own sake, not for the good of himself and other rulers.

[64] *Ibid.*, B. I, c. 10.
[65] *Ibid.*, B. I, c. 11.
[66] Eppstein, John, *The Catholic Tradition of the Law of Nations,* London: Burns Oates & Washbourne, 1935, p. 287.

Therefore the human race existing under a Monarch is best ordered, and from this it follows that a Monarchy is essential to the well-being of the world.[67]

8. The Monarch is most capable of ruling, in fact, is alone capable of the supreme qualifications necessary to rule, since "a Monarch can have no occasion for cupidity, or rather less occasion than any other men, even other princes, and cupidity is the sole corrupter of judgment and hindrance to Justice."

It was rightly assumed, then, that the Monarch alone is capable of supreme qualification to rule. Hence the Monarch is best able to direct others. Therefore it follows that for the best ordering of the world, Monarchy is necessary.[68]

9. Whatever can be accomplished by one agent is better than by many. Dante elaborates this argument by showing that unity of wills is necessary for the peace and harmony of mankind, but seems to argue conveniently to his own purpose when he asserts that this unity of wills is impossible "unless there is one common Prince whose will may dominate and guide the wills of all others."[69]

10. As a confirmation of the preceding arguments, Dante regards the birth of Christ in the Empire of Caesar Augustus as the stamp of divine approval on the idea of a single world Monarchy for the whole human race.[70]

That the arguments deduced by Dante actually confirm his thesis for the necessity of a single world Monarch is questionable. But they do furnish valuable principles to prove the proposition that the human race possesses a certain unity and that all men, regardless of race and nationality, should form a single, organic, world society. Dante, at least if his words are taken literally, failed to make the important distinction between a single world society and a single world ruler. As Eppstein remarks:

[67] Dante, *op. cit.*, B. I, c. 12.
[68] *Ibid.*, B. I, c. 13.
[69] *Ibid.*, B. I, c. 15.
[70] *Ibid.*, B. I, c. 16.

Two propositions—by an association of thought natural at the time—are confused in the mind of Dante Alighieri as he develops his thesis upon the necessity of monarchy. The first is that the nature of man and the common good of peoples require a single government for the world; the second that the form of that government must necessarily be the rule of a single man.[71]

The contention is made by some writers that Dante's Monarch is simply a personification of universal rule or government by law. But such an interpretation seems to be forcing the obvious meaning of Dante's words in an attempt to modernize them and to harmonize them with our present international convictions. Thus Beales writes:

But by the rule of the Emperor Dante meant the rule of Law. His word Monarch connoted government. The actual personal sovereign was only an official, removable if he proved unfaithful to the sovereign people. Law was "the rule which directs life." . . . The organization of the world, in a word, should be a universal Empire based on a universal Law.[72]

That the universal rule of the world Monarch was to be a rule of law and justice is certainly true. Justice, law, and order form the only firm basis for the universal peace so earnestly desired by Dante. But the universal Empire was to be the rule of a personal Monarch who would govern mankind, not according to mere caprice, but according to law and justice.

The remedy for the unrest and disorder of his time, as Dante dreamed, lay in the universal Empire. Before his eyes there unfolded itself a bright vision, in which the supreme Monarch, high above the smaller states and their rulers, exercised a system of law and justice and order to which all the petty kings and governments must submit.[73]

[71] Eppstein, *op. cit.*, p. 278.

[72] Beales, A. C. F., *The History of Peace*, New York: Dial Press, 1931, p. 24.

[73] Ramsay, W. M., *The Imperial Peace — An Ideal in European History*, Oxford: at the Clarendon Press, 1913, p. 6.

As a plea for a universal and organic world society based on law and order, justice and charity, Dante's *De Monarchia* still retains much of its original cogency. But as an apology for the Holy Roman Empire, which was its primary objective, Dante's book, to quote Lord Bryce, "is an epitaph instead of a prophecy."[74]

Dante's *De Monarchia* was the epitaph, not only of the Holy Roman Empire, but of the idea of a universal world Empire as well. After Dante's time, to be sure, apologies for the Empire continued to appear, such as that of Engelbert d'Admont, *De ortu et fine Romani imperii*, and the *Defensor Pacis*, written in 1324 by Marsilius of Padua and John of Jandun. The latter, however, was concerned, not with universal peace and world rule, but with the necessity of the Empire's independence from the Church.[75] Throughout the remainder of the Middle Ages and up until modern times the dream of a universal Empire continued to exert its appeal, though in an ever diminishing degree, upon the minds of men. As late as the sixteenth century we find this manifested in a work written by James Antonius of Cambrai entitled, *Elegans libellus . . . de praecellentia potestatis imperatoris* (1502).[76]

B. PROPOSALS FOR AN INTERNATIONAL ORGANIZATION
OF SOVEREIGN AND INDEPENDENT STATES—
FROM THE LATE MIDDLE AGES UNTIL EARLY MODERN TIMES

1. *Pierre Dubois*

Three great currents of thought dominated the European political scene in the early fourteenth century: 1. the redemption of the Holy Land, which after numerous frustrated attempts still remained the great objective for the crusading spirit of Christian Europe and which served as a

[74] Bryce, *op. cit.*, p. 264.
[75] Lange, *op. cit.*, pp. 76-77.
[76] Nys, Ernest, *Les origines du droit international*, Brussels: Alfred Castaigne, 1894, p. 43.

strong bond of unification among the peoples of Christendom; 2. the desire for peace in the Christian world, always considered as the necessary predisposition for a successful Crusade; 3. the new national ideas which gave the impetus to the formation of national, sovereign, and indepedent states.[77]

These currents of thought are all reflected in a unique work, *De Recuperatione Terre Sancte*, "On the Recovery of the Holy Land," written about the year 1306 by Pierre Dubois, a contemporary of Dante, and a student of St. Thomas Aquinas at the University of Paris, who later became a jurist and personal advocate of Philip the Fair, King of France. As is suggested by the title, the primary objective of this work was the presentation of a plan for the organization of a Crusade to regain the Holy Land. As such, the work is not really significant, for it represented but one of many similar plans current at the time.

What is really significant in this work, however, is that as a necessary condition for the successful undertaking of a Crusade, Dubois presented a plan for the pacification and unification of Europe which advocated for the first time a federation of sovereign and independent Christian states.[78] This proposal of Dubois contained the necessary elements for a genuine international society: 1. guarantees for peace within Christendom, 2. a federation of independent and sovereign nations, 3. an international court of arbitration, 4. the enforcement of sanctions, 5. a final court of appeal in the Holy See.[79]

The assurance of universal peace within Christendom is the first and indispensable prerequisite for the organization of a Crusade against the Infidel. All wars between Christian states must be banished; Christian rulers must be completely united at home before attempting to accomplish their objective abroad.[80]

---

[77] Meulen, *op. cit.*, I, p. 83.

[78] Beales, *op. cit.*, p. 23.   [79] Meulen, *op. cit.*, I, p. 102.

[80] Ad hoc quod tanta multitudo ducatur illuc [the Holy Land] et duret, opportebit principes catholicos concordes esse et inter se guer-

In order to insure peace among Christian rulers, Dubois proposed a plan for a society or federation of Christian states, which would function through a Congress (*Concilium*) composed of the rulers of these states, or their representatives, and of ecclesiastical prelates, the representatives of the Church. It was the idea of the Ecumenical Council, adapted to the exigencies of the Christian political world. The states to be represented in the Congress or Council are not the vassal states of an Empire, but sovereign and independent Christian states. Dubois states this explicitly: the Congress is to be composed of "those states and rulers who do not recognize any superiors [temporal] above them on the earth."[81]

Dubois therefore championed the cause of the new Nationalism, but at the same time realized its repercussions on the relations between nations and on the solidarity of Christendom. He wanted to find some new principle, which, while assuring the existence of independent and sovereign states, would nevertheless guarantee their coexistence in peace and harmony.[82] He was therefore the first to offer a definite plan for the unification of Christian political communities, not in the form of an Empire, but as a society of national, sovereign, and independent states.

Yet, as Schücking observes, while championing the cause of Nationalism, Dubois was none the less truly a man of the Middle Ages. That Christendom should be one political unit, not only in theory but in fact, he took for granted; it

---

ras non habere.... Idcirco inter catholicos omnes, saltem ecclesie romane obedientes, pacem firmari taliter expedit quod una sit respublica, sic fortiter unita quod non dividatur.—Dubois, Pierre, *De Recuperatione Terre Sancte*, in Meulen, *op. cit.*, I, 102. (All direct quotations are cited from the text given by Meulen).

[81] ... sed cum iste civitates et multi principes superiores in terris non recognoscentes.... — *Ibid.*, I, p. 104.

... vocatis praelatis et principibus catholicis sibi [Papae] obedientibus, praesertim regibus et aliis qui non recognoscunt superiores in terris.... — *Ibid.*, I, 103. (In the Congress the Holy Roman Emperor would be considered simply as one of these sovereign rulers).

[82] Lange, *op. cit.*, p. 101.

is the will of God that all should live in peace and harmony. And since he felt that the universal Empire or Monarchy was an impossible and impractical means of securing the unity of Christendom, the various Christian states, while retaining their sovereignty and independence, must be united through some form of international organization. Dubois found the pattern for such an organization in the General Council of the Church, an international assembly of a true international society of the spiritual order, and adapted it to the exigencies of the political order. In this Dubois shows the influence of the Church, as well as in the prominent rôle which he assigns to the Pope and prelates of the Church in the Congress of Nations.[83] Yet, it may also be remarked that the work of Dubois likewise gives evidence of the contemporary controversy between Philip the Fair, King of France, and Pope Boniface VIII and of the author's allegiance to his political master, Philip the Fair: the Congress of Nations advocated by Dubois was to be convened indeed by the Pope, but only at the request of Philip the Fair, and was to be held near Toulouse, in French territory.

A brief outline of Dubois' plan will suffice to indicate its essential features. All particular details of organization may be omitted.

1. All Christian states should be united in a single society, the *Respublica Christiana*, functioning through a Congress (*Concilium*) composed of sovereign Christian rulers (or their representatives) and prelates of the Church. The Congress shall be summoned by the Pope, at the request of the King of France. The place of the Congress is to be near Toulouse in France.[84]

---

[83] Schücking, *op. cit.*, p. 29.

[84] ... videtur expediens supplicare domino pape quod ipse citra montes, super his vocatis praelatis et principibus catholicis sibi obedientibus, praesertim regibus et aliis qui non recognoscunt superiores in terris, Concilium faciat generale.... — Dubois, *op. cit.*, in Meulen, *op. cit.*, I, p. 103.

2.   In the Congress the Pope will hold the first rank.   It will be his right to introduce in the first instance proposals for the consideration of the assembly.[85]

3.   An international tribunal or court of justice will be set up by the Congress.   It will be the function of this court to decide all disputes between sovereign rulers or states. The court will consist of a panel of six judges, three clerical and three lay, all of upright character and skilled in law, who will meet as a body for the decision of any issue referred to it.[86]   The object of this measure is the substitution of peaceful means for war in the solution of difficulties arising between Christian rulers.   It is a positive effort to eliminate internal warfare within Christendom, with a view, of course, to the necessity of such peace and unity for the organization of a successful Crusade.

4.   Sanctions will be invoked by the Congress against offenders who break the peace or who refuse to abide by the decision of the Court.   Such offenders are to be deprived of all possessions, and, together with all living relatives, are to be banished to the Holy Land.[87]

[85] The expression "videtur expediens, quod summus pontifex in Concilio statuat" is found frequently in the text of Dubois.—Meulen, *op. cit.*, I, p. 103.

[86] Sed cum iste civitates et multi principes superiores in terris non recognoscentes, qui justiciam faciant de ipsis secundum leges et consuetudines locorum, controversias movere captabunt, coram quibus precedent et litigabunt?   Responderi potest quod concilium statuat arbitros religiosos aut alios eligendos, viros prudentes et expertos ac fideles, qui jurati tres judices praelatos et tres alios pro utraque parte ... diligentissime examinent. ... — *Ibid.*, I, p. 104. Although Dubois is very explicit in all the details of the judicial procedure before the tribunal, in which he gives evidence of his legal profession, he is not clear as to the manner in which the tribunal itself, the panel of six judges, is to be selected in each instance.   It is possible that Dubois meant that the Congress should appoint a number of eligible judges, six of whom would be selected in each particular controversy.   But as to the person or parties making this selection, the text of Dubois has been interpreted in various ways by different authors.   cf. Schücking, *op. cit.*, p. 29; Lange, *op. cit.*, pp. 103-105.

[87] Meulen, *op. cit.*, I, pp. 103-105.

5. Yet if one of the parties to the controversy is not satisfied with the decision of the Court, an appeal may be made from the Court to the Pope.[88]   This provision for a single supreme judge as the ultimate court of appeal, in the opinion of Lange, weakens the authority of Dubois' international court to such an extent that it becomes merely a fact-finding commission, the decisions of which become authoritative only upon confirmation by the Pope, and that furthermore it involves a contradiction to the fundamental principle of his project, the principle of national sovereignty: he proposes an organization of sovereign rulers "who recognize no superior on earth," and ends by placing above them a superior, the Pope, whom they must all recognize as supreme judge.[89]   However, this apparent contradiction loses much of its force when it is remembered that Dubois assumes that all Christian sovereign rulers recognize the Pope as their spiritual, though not their temporal, superior, and that the decision of a dispute between rulers is ultimately a matter of justice, of morality, which lies within the province of the Pope's spiritual authority.

In spite of its advanced proposals, the plan of Dubois exerted little or no influence on the international situation of his time.   It has assumed a significant place in the history of international projects, but in actual European history it played little part.   The reason why the plan of Dubois failed to influence contemporary conditions is, says Schücking, precisely because it was too advanced for the times. The idea of the Empire was still too strong at that period, even though the Holy Roman Empire was declining in power, to be replaced all at once by the essential equality of

---

[88] Si altera pars de ipsorum non sit contenta, ipsi judices pro omni lite processus cum sententiis mittant ad apostolicam sedem per summum pontificem pro tempore existentem emendandas et mutandas, prout et si justum fuerit; vel, si non, salubriter ad perpetuam rei memoriam confirmandas et in cronicis sancte romane ecclesie inregistrandas. *Ibid.*, I, p. 106.

[89] Lange, *op. cit.*, pp. 105-106.

independent sovereign states, upon which the project of Dubois was based.[90]

In fact, Dubois himself was not always consistent with this principle. His internationalism was marred by an exaggerated nationalism which went even to the extreme of the universal imperialism he had opposed so vigorously in his international project. There were two sides to Dubois' political thought and aspirations: at times he was a far-sighted realist who realized the necessity of some form of international organization among sovereign states; at other times he was an ardent nationalist and dreamer who envisioned France as the leader of the world and Philip the Fair as the universal emperor. Even his book, *De Recuperatione Terre Sancte*, reveals these two aspects of his thought. It consists of two parts: the first contains his international plan and was addressed by Dubois to the Pope, the King of England, and other rulers, as well as to the King of France; the second part, written solely for the King of France, advocated French supremacy in Europe, suggested means for achieving this end, and urged Philip the Fair to acquire for himself and his family the title of Emperor.[91] But it would be unfair to Dubois to condemn his international proposal as simply a disguise to establish the hegemony of France over Europe. Although Dubois expected France to take a leading part in the organization of the *Respublica Christiana*, there is good reason to think that he really had at heart the unity and peace of Christendom. His proposal for achieving this end remains as the first plan on record for the organization of an international society of sovereign, independent, and equal states.[92]

2. *George Podiebrad, King of Bohemia*

A century and a half after Dubois had devised his plan, another proposal for an international organization was addressed to the rulers of Europe. In the meantime tremen-

[90] Schücking, *op. cit.*, p. 30.   [91] Meulen, *op. cit.*, I, pp. 106-107.
[92] Lange, *op. cit.*, p. 100. Beales, *op. cit.*, p. 23.

dous changes had taken place within Europe. The political unity of Europe was weakened by the coming to power of rival national states, which waged almost ceaseless war on one another, as exemplified by the Hundred Years' War between England and France. The religious unity of Christendom too was threatened by the Great Western Schism and the beginning of religious revolutions under Wyclif and Hus. The relation of Europe with the outside world had changed diametrically: in the time of Dubois, Christian Europe took the offensive in the organization of Crusades against the Infidels for the rescue of the Holy Land; at this time, Europe was on the defensive. The Turks had developed into a great military power, had already conquered the Eastern Empire, and were threatening to overrun Central and Western Europe. It was necessary for Christendom to fight for its own existence. It was this danger of Turkish invasion which proved the most effective external incentive to the political unity of Christendom during the fifteenth century, just as the Crusades had done during the later Middle Ages.

To meet this danger of Turkish invasion (Constantinople had fallen to the Turks in 1453), George Podiebrad, King of Bohemia, with the assistance of his adviser, Antonius Marini, a French industrialist from Grenoble, drew up a plan for the organization of the Christian rulers of Europe into a single Union or Federation. The immediate objective of this plan was the unification of Christian states, with a view to the ultimate objective, the common defense of Christendom against the Turks. The details of the project were set forth in a work composed by Marini, at the instance of the King, bearing the title *De Unione Christianorum contra Turcas*. In 1463 George Podiebrad sent Marini as his personal representative to various European rulers to interest them in his project for the organization of Christendom. But neither the Pope nor the Emperor were included in the mission of Marini. The omission of the Pope is easily explained: Podiebrad was a follower of Hus and consequently a heretic who professed no allegiance to the Pope. His

exclusion of the Pope, not only from the consideration of his
plan, but also from any part in his proposed organization,
placed a purely secular stamp on Podiebrad's whole project.[93] The fact that the Emperor received no recognition
other than that of a German King is explicable if one considers the nature of the project itself, and possibly also the
personal political ambitions of its author, which will be
referred to later.

George Podiebrad introduced his plan by recalling the
former glory, great power, and prosperous condition of a
once-united Christendom. Once there were numerous
flourishing Christian kingdoms; many of these were now
in the hands of the infidel Mohammed and the "detestable
Turks."[94]

The first and all important step in remedying this situation is the restoration of unity to Christendom. Although
Podiebrad was a heretic and excluded the spiritual head of
Christendom, the Pope, from his considerations, he nevertheless retained some semblance of the mediaeval notion of
the unity of Christendom, and even declared that one can
engage in no more noble work than that of effecting peace
and unity among Christian nations and defending the faith
of Christ against the Turks.[95]

For the achievement of peace and unity among Christian

---

[93] Schücking, *op. cit.*, p. 33.

[94] In nomine Domini nostri Jesus Christi; Nos, Georgius, Rex Bo-
hemiae, notum facimus universis et singulis ad perpetuam rei memoriam quod dum veterum historicorum scripta recensemus, reperi-
mus Christianitatem florentissimam quondam fuisse et hominibus,
opibusque beatam, cujus tanta longetudo, latitudoque fuit, ut in ejus
ventre centum decem et septem regna amplissima clauderentur....
—*De Unione Christianorum contra Turcas*, in Meulen, *op. cit.*, I, pp.
110-111. (All direct quotations are cited from the text given by
Meulen.)

[95] Scimus quod sanctimoniae nostrae nihil religiosius, integritati nil
congruentius et laudi nil gloriosius efficere poterimus, quam dare
operam quod vera, pura et firma pax, unio et charitas inter christianos
fiat, et fides Christi adversus immanissimum Turchum defensetur.—
Ibid., I, p. 111.

rulers, certain measures were designated by Podiebrad as essential:

1.   All Christian rulers must enter into a mutual treaty and establish a union or federation.

2.   All members of the union must pledge mutual aid and assistance in case of an attack, either from within or without.

3.   War must be banished between all members of the federation.

4.   Sanctions must be invoked against all offenders; such sanctions are to be moral, in the first instance, but military, if necessary.[96]

The explanation of the purpose of the Federation and the necessary means of action, indicated above, constitutes the first part of Podiebrad's (or Marini's) work; the second part deals with the organization or constitution of the Federation. Although the author is not always consistent and explicit in the use of his terms, it would seem that the organization outlined in the project could be reduced to the following three elements:

1.   A general assembly (*Congregatio* or *Collegium*) consisting of the representatives of sovereign Christian states.

2.   A special council (*Speciale Concilium*).

3.   An international court (*Consistorium Parlamentum,* or *Judicium*).

Because of its importance, attention was given first to the establishment of a court or tribunal as the judicial organ of the Federation. Since justice is bound up intimately with peace, provisions must be made to secure justice for all, rulers and subjects, in their relations with one another.[97] For this reason, it is necessary in the first instance to set up a court which will have jurisdiction over the members of the Federation in their relations with one another. The

---

[96] *Ibid.,* I, pp. 111-114.

[97] Verum cum pacis cultus a justitia et justitia ab illo esse non possit, et per justitiam pax gignitur et conservatur, nec sine illa nos et subditi nostri in pace subsistere poterimus, ob id rei paci justitiam annectimus.... — *Ibid.,* I, p. 116.

personnel and the specific functions of the court are to be determined by the General Assembly (*Congregatio*) either unanimously or by majority vote.[98]

The General Assembly (*Congregatio, Collegium,* or *Universitas*) will be composed of the representatives of all rulers who are parties to the treaty constituting them members of the Federation. Provision is made for the incorporation of future members also. The Assembly is to be permanent in nature, but will meet in various cities; it will convene first at Basel and remain there for a period of five years, after which it will meet in some chosen city in each of the member states until the round has been completely made. The idea of a rotating assembly was borrowed, no doubt, from the Council of Constance.[99]

The method of voting in the Assembly is interesting in that it manifests the growing trend of nationalistic distinctions. The members are to be classified according to nationality and are to be divided into national groups: French, German, Italian, Spanish. Each of these national groups is to possess a single cumulative vote. If there is no unanimity, issues are to be decided by majority vote.[100]

In addition to the General Assembly there is to be also a special Council (*Speciale Concilium*) but nothing further is stated regarding its nature, purpose, and functions. The Assembly will have as its leader a "presiding Father and Head."[101]

---

[98] ... praevidimus primitus ordinare quoddam generale Consistorium quod omnium nostrorum et totius Congregationis nostrae nomine in loco ubi Congregatio ipsa pro tempore fuerit observetur, a quo velut a fonte justitiae undique deriventur. Quod quidem judicium ordinabitur in numero et qualitate personarum et statutorum prout subscripta nostra Congregatio vel major pars ejusdem concluserit et decreverit.—*Ibid.,* I, p. 116.

[99] *Ibid.,* I, p. 118.

[100] *Ibid.,* I, p. 119.

[101] ... unumquoque proprium et speciale concilium ipsa Congregatio habeat; unus praesidens Pater et Caput N. et nos coeteri Christianitatis Reges et Principes membra simus.—*Ibid.,* I, p. 118.

This "presiding Father and Head" is to be neither the Emperor nor the Pope. As has already been mentioned, the Pope was almost completely excluded from the organization of Podiebrad. Indeed, he is "assigned" certain extra-conciliar functions, such as maintaining peace among those who are not members of the Federation and punishing offenders with spiritual penalties. But the Pope is not even numbered among the representatives of the Italian nation, in spite of the size and influence of the Papal States at the time. Yet he is to encourage the Italian people to equip a fleet for a campaign against the Turks and is to divert Church revenues to that purpose![102]

The Holy Roman Emperor was likewise brushed aside by Podiebrad. He was to be included in the Federation, to be sure, but simply in the capacity of a German king, not as Emperor. Here was a project destined by its very nature to eliminate the notion of Empire completely; there was no mention of Empire and Emperor, but only of Nations and Kings. The details of Podiebrad's plan give a clear indication of the extent to which the ideal of the Middle Ages had by this time disintegrated.[103]

It is the opinion of Schücking that this very exclusion of the Emperor, and especially of the Pope, constituted the essential weakness of Podiebrad's project. For just at this period there was a resurgence in the power of the Holy Roman Empire under Emperor Sigismund. And the Papacy continued to exert its far-reaching influence over all of Christian Europe which had not yet been divided by the Protestant Reformation.[104] It was precisely because of the exclusion of the Pope that Marini, when presenting Podiebrad's plan, failed to receive any consideration from such Catholic rulers as Philip of Burgundy and the Doge of Venice. In fact, the only practical result achieved by Marini was the signing of a pact of mutual friendship between George Podiebrad, King of Bohemia, and Louis XI, King of France. Indeed, Lange expresses the suspicion that

---

[102] Schücking, *op. cit.*, p. 34.   [103] *Ibid.*, p. 33.   [104] *Ibid.*, p. 34.

the whole project of Podiebrad was a purely political scheme by which the King of Bohemia and the King of France could secure the complete domination of Europe. And for this reason the project merited the failure and the oblivion to which it was condemned.[105]

But whatever may be said of Podiebrad's motives, this much is true, as Lange also notes: his plan is both interesting and worthy of attention in that it presents clearly and precisely a problem which has never ceased to trouble Europe to this day, namely, the peaceful coordination of sovereign and independent states.[106]

The project of Podiebrad was the last detailed proposal for the unification of European states until the seventeenth century. Pope Leo X, it is true, in 1517 attempted the organization of European rulers for a campaign against the Turks, assembled a convention of Cardinals and representatives of Christian states, and proclaimed a five year armistice between Christian rulers, but his efforts to effect a permanent organization were nullified by the intrigues of Wolsey, Chancellor of England, and the indifference and opposition of European rulers generally.[107] After Leo X all hopes of establishing a single European confederation of states under the leadership of the Papacy were entirely blasted. In fact, the hopes for the complete unification of Europe under any form of leadership, save that of military domination, all but vanished. For the year 1517 also marked the beginning of the period in the history of international organization which Schücking appropriately calls the "Era of Disorganization." It was this year 1517 which marked the beginning of the Protestant Revolt or Reformation which dissolved the religious unity of Christendom, gave the death blow to that political unity which still sur-

[105] Lange, *op. cit.*, p. 117.

[106] Le projet a donc mérité l'oubli complet auquel il a été condamné. Il a cependant son intérêt par ce qu'il posa nettement un problème qui n'a cessé de s'imposer depuis: la coordination dans la paix des états souverains de l'Europe.—*Ibid.*, p. 117.

[107] Meulen, *op. cit.*, I, pp. 129-139.

vived from the Middle Ages, and, by accentuating religious and national differences, forced a cleavage between the various states of Europe which was remained to the present time.[108]

As a reaction to the chaotic condition following the religious revolt of the sixteenth century, numerous proposals for the establishment of peace and the organization of an international society appeared during the seventeenth and eighteenth centuries. The most famous of these projects are: the "Grand Design" of Henry IV, King of France, developed and recorded by the Duc de Sully in his *Memoires*, written between 1617 and 1638; the *Nouveau Cynée* of Émeric Crucé, a French Carmelite Friar, published in 1623, which is significant in that it advocated for the first time a federation including non-Christian as well as Christian states; William Penn's plan for the establishment of a "European Parliament" (1693); Abbé de St. Pierre's "Project for a Perpetual Peace" (1716); Jean Jacques Rousseau's "Lasting Peace through the Federation of Europe" (1761); Immanuel Kant's essay on "Perpetual Peace" (1795); and Jeremy Bentham's plan for "A Universal and Perpetual Peace" (1786 or 1789). But it was not until the nineteenth century that these ideas were given any concrete form, beginning with the "Holy Alliance" in 1815 and culminating with the Covenant of the League of Nations in 1919. It had seemed that, with the signing of this Covenant by the majority of the nations of the world, the ideal of an international society, not only for Europe, but for the whole

[108] Mit der Reformation aber geht dann jener ungeheure Riss durch die Christenheit, und dem zunächst jede internationale Organisation, in welcher Form auch immer, scheitern muss. Und so fruchtbringend die Reformation für die geistige Kultur der Neuzeit geworden, eines werden wir immer beklagen müssen, dass nämlich das einheitliche Kulturbewusstsein der Christenheit, die Idee der Zusammengehörigkeit der abendländischen Kultur durch die Glaubensspaltung, für Jahrhunderte verloren gehen sollte. Die Zersetzung der einheiltlichen Welt des Mittelalters, vorbereitet durch die politischen Wandlungen der letzten Jahrhunderte, ist durch die Reformation vollendet.—Schücking, *op. cit.*, p. 37.

world, had been finally and permanently realized. But the fate of the League of Nations in the turmoil of the present world conflict reminds us all too vividly that we are still in the "Era of Disorganization."

For the purposes of this treatise it will not be necessary to carry the consideration of these proposals of international organization any further. The project of Podiebrad brings us up to the threshold of modern times, coming within a half-century of the Protestant Reformation. The plans of Dubois and Podiebrad have been treated at some length, not because they manifest any profound ethical doctrine or theory of international relations, but rather because they are contemporary witnesses to the gradual change in political thinking and action from the mediaeval ideal of the universal Christian Empire to the modern concept of independent and sovereign national states. Both of these projects were based on the fundamental principle of national sovereignty. Both were attempts to solve the problem which follows immediately upon the application of this principle, namely, the problem of coordinating these equally sovereign and independent states in order to assure their coexistence in peace and unity.

It is to the consideration of this problem that the present treatise is devoted. We shall not be concerned, however, with the specific plans proposed during the past centuries for the organization of an international society within Europe or for the whole world. Rather, the problem will be considered from the particular view point of the basic philosophical principles which should underlie any form of organization which purports to be a genuine society of nations. These basic principles are drawn from the philosophy of St. Thomas Aquinas, formulated in the thirteenth century by the greatest of Catholic philosophers, developed by the followers of St. Thomas, and, applied particularly to international relations in the sixteenth century by the eminent Spanish Thomist, Francisco de Vitoria.

CHAPTER II

THE NATURAL BASIS OF
INTERNATIONAL SOCIETY

Every human society must be based firmly and objectively on the nature and end of man. Apart from man, society has no meaning. This is a cardinal principle of all Thomistic social and political philosophy. If international society is to have a solid foundation, it too must be based objectively on human nature and the end of man. International society is, in fact, the final terminus in the natural order of the basic social principles enunciated by St. Thomas Aquinas and elaborated by later Thomists. It is the purpose of this chapter to review these social principles and to show how their logical and progressive development leads to the concept of an international society.

In Thomistic philosophy, family, state, and international society form one complete and unified social pattern. These are progressive stages in the development of the same fundamental natural social tendencies in human nature which St. Thomas had in mind when he described man as an *animal naturaliter sociale*.[1] This total view of human society has been well expressed by St. Augustine: "After the state or city comes the world, the third circle of human society,— the first being the home, and the second the city."[2] The total social order of mankind involves every natural society ranging from the family to international society, each being a more complete development and manifestation of the same basic social tendencies intrinsic to human nature itself. As a basis for the synthetic study of this complete social order, it will be necessary to begin with an analysis of man as a social being or as a constituent of society.

I. MAN

From the social point of view, man, as a constituent of society, should be considered both in himself and in his re-

[1] *Summa Theologica*, I, q. 96, a. 4.
[2] St. Augustine, *De Civitate Dei*, XIX, c. 7.

lations to others. Considered in himself, man is an organic composite of matter and spirit, possessing a material body and a rational soul. Both the material and spiritual elements are important, and likewise their conjunction to form the complete human being; such is the notion of man which St. Thomas took from Aristotle and made the basis of his own teaching. Man is neither wholly matter, nor wholly spirit, but an organic union of both.[3] Although insistence on this point might seem to be laboring the obvious, it is of the utmost importance to have at the very outset a true conception of man, for only upon such a basis can a genuine theory of society be developed which will avoid the extremes of an excessive spiritualism and, what is much more prevalent today, a theory of society based on crass materialism.

Because of his material element, man has numerous material needs in common with all other animals. This is too evident to require any elaboration; the social implications of this fact, however, are far-reaching, as will be seen when the relations of man to his fellowmen are considered. But it is the spiritual principle in man which differentiates man from all other animals. It is this spiritual principle which makes man an intelligent and free agent, a person, which, as St. Thomas says, "signifies that which is most perfect in all nature."[4] It is precisely because man is a person, a rational creature endowed with intelligence and free will, that he alone among all the animals is capable of striving consciously and freely for the proper end of his existence. All creatures indeed strive for the end of their existence imparted to them by the Creator, but only rational creatures are capable of directing themselves consciously and freely to their proper end. On this distinction St. Thomas is very explicit:

> Those things that lack reason tend to an end by natural inclination, as being moved by another and not by themselves, since they do not know by an-

[3] *Summa Theol.*, I, q. 75, a. 4.
[4] Persona significat id quod est perfectissimum in tota natura; scilicet, subsistens in rationali natura.—*Ibid.*, I, q. 29, a. 3.

other and not by themselves, since they do not
know the nature of an end as such, and consequently cannot ordain anything to an end, but can be ordained to an end only by another.... Consequently
it is proper to the rational nature to tend to an end
as directing and leading itself to the end; whereas
it is proper to the irrational creature to tend to an
end as directed or led by another....[5]

Since man is a rational creature, capable of self-direction
towards his proper end, he also has the ability to understand
and the obligation to choose the means necessary for the
achievement for that end. It is for this reason that man
has certain primary duties as well as certain fundamental
rights which are indispensable conditions for attaining the
end of his existence. Thus it is the concept of end or final
cause which is the key to the whole doctrine of St. Thomas
on man. If, indeed, the entire philosophical system of St.
Thomas is teleological, this is especially true of his moral
and social philosophy. That St. Thomas intended to give an
objective, teleological basis to his whole system of social
and political philosophy is evident from the opening paragraphs of his *ex professo* treatise on government, *De Regimine Principum,* in which he appeals to the end of man as
his first principle and starting point:

In all things which are ordered towards some
end, wherein this or that course may be adopted,
some directive principle is needed through which
the due end may be reached by the most direct
route....
Now, man has an end to which his whole life and
all his actions are ordered; for man is an intelli-

---

[5] Illa vero quae ratione carent, tendunt in finem propter naturalem
inclinationem, quasi ab alio mota, non autem a seipsis, cum non cog-
noscant rationem finis; et ideo nihil in finem ordinare possunt, sed
solum in finem ab alio ordinantur.... Et ideo proprium est naturae
rationalis, ut tendat in finem, quasi se agens, vel ducens ad finem;
naturae vero irrationalis, quasi ab alio acta, vel ducta....— *Summa
Theologica,* I, II, q. 1, a. 2. English translation by English Dominican
Fathers, London: Burns Oates and Washbourne; New York: Benziger, 1911-1922, vol. VI, p. 5.

gent agent, and it is clearly the part of an intelligent agent to act in view of an end.[6]

The end of man is the guiding principle throughout the entire synthesis of Thomistic social and political philosophy. Its importance cannot be overstated; it is the end of man which gives society its meaning, and it is in the light of this guiding principle of finality that the solution of all social problems is sought. It is of the utmost importance for a philosophy of society that the end of man be designated in precise and definite terms, not merely in vague generalities. According to St. Thomas, the end of man is two-fold: ultimate and immediate. The ultimate end of man is not to be found in man himself, but in God, the beginning and end of his existence; hence, man's ultimate end is not attainable in this present temporal life, but is other-worldly, supermundane, and consists in the possession of God, which is at the same time for man perfect and eternal beatitude. The immediate end of man is that for which he must strive in this present life: temporal happiness, which consists principally in a life of virtue. This immediate end is the means and preparation for the ultimate end; it is through living virtuously that man attains to the possession of God.[7] For man to achieve his immediate end, namely, temporal happiness through a life of virtue, not only are knowledge and moral goodness required, but also a sufficiency of material goods.[8] Although these material goods stand lowest in the hierarchy of goods or values, being superseded by goods of the body, such as health and integrity of the bodily members, and still more by the goods of the soul, such as knowledge and moral virtue, yet they are necessary as instru-

[6] In omnibus autem quae ad finem aliquem ordinantur, in quibus contingit sic et aliter procedere, opus est aliquo dirigente, per quod directe debitum perveniatur ad finem ... hominis autem est aliquis finis, ad quem tota vita ejus et actio ordinatur, cum sit agens per intellectum, cujus est manifeste propter finem operari.—*De Regimine Principum*, Lib. I, cap. 1. English translation by Gerald B. Phelan, Toronto: St. Michael's College, 1935; New York: Sheed and Ward, 1938.

[7] *Ibid.*, Lib. I, cap. 14.   [8] *Ibid.*, Lib. I, cap. 15.

ments both for the preservation of the body and for the acquisition of such spiritual goods as knowledge and virtue.[9] From this analysis of man and his end St. Thomas deduces a scale of values or goods which he applies to society as a whole as well as to the individual man. It is thus that St. Thomas lays the foundation for his teaching on society, which is as distinctively human as it is thoroughly objective.

It is likewise from the nature and end of man, considered in relation to his fellowmen, that St. Thomas deduced the fundamental fact of man's sociability. As an organic composite of body and soul, man has material as well as spiritual needs; the normal and natural method of satisfying these needs is through the medium of relationships with other men. Thus there is in man a natural inclination to associate with other men and to seek their assistance; it is this that Aristotle has in mind when he designates man as a "political animal,"[10] and St. Thomas when he calls man a "social" as well as a "political animal."[11] Although the fact of man's sociability was a matter of every-day experience for St. Thomas as it was for Aristotle, yet he realized that

[9] *Summa Theol.*, II, II, q. 73, a. 3; *De Reg. Prin.*, Lib. I, cap. 15.

[10] Aristotle, *Politics*, Book I, chap. 2, 1253a.

[11] *Contra Gentiles*, III, cap. 85. It may be noted while Aristotle used the single term "political animal" ($\pi o \lambda \iota \tau \iota \kappa \grave{o} \nu \ \zeta \tilde{\omega} o \nu$) to designate this natural propensity in man to associate with his fellowmen, especially in political society, St. Thomas added the term *animal sociale* to *animal politicum* of Aristotle. Sometimes he used the two terms in conjunction, but more frequently he used either one or the other. Of the two terms, *animal sociale* appears in many more passages than does the corresponding *animale politicum*. It is possible that St. Thomas meant to call attention to the fact that this social inclination is operative in man from the very beginning, prior to the formation of political society. Hence, the opinion has been advanced that St. Thomas used these two terms, not to express identically the same thing, nor on the other hand two different inclinations in man, but rather to designate two manifestations or stages of development of the one and same inclination in man to associate with his fellowmen, first, in simple social groups, and secondly in the more complex political society. cf. Meyer, Hans, *Thomas von Aquin*, Bonn: Peter Hanstein, 1938, p. 473, note 1.

it cannot be adequately explained without reference to man's rational nature and the end of his existence. What distinguishes human sociability from the gregariousness of the lower animals is rationality; while the latter move instinctively towards the end imparted to them by the Creator, "the light of reason is placed by nature in every man, to guide him in his acts towards his end."[12] While there are certain physical needs which are common to both man and the lower animals, namely, those required for the preservation of the individual and the propagation of the species, yet the manner of satisfying these needs varies according to the nature of each; irrational animals seek the means of satisfying these needs instinctively, while in the case of man reason predominates. But since man is a rational being, endowed with intelligence and free will, he also has needs of a higher order, intellectual and moral needs, which likewise require satisfaction if he is to attain the full development and perfection of all his natural faculties. Normally, this can be accomplished only by the cooperation of one man with another. Thus we find among men a three-fold interdependence: material, intellectual, and moral.

The physical interdependence of mankind is a fact of common experience as well as of history. The earliest records of mankind as well as anthropological researches among primitive peoples of the present day depict everywhere men living in social groups for the purpose of mutual assistance in the satisfaction of their common needs. Neither history nor prehistory furnish any evidence of a state of nature in which man lived as an isolated individualist, either as the warring monster of Hobbes, or as the perfect, contented, self-sufficient animal of Rousseau. Sound social and political thinkers, on the contrary, have always insisted on the fact of man's natural interdependence in the

---

[12] Est autem unicuique hominum naturaliter insitum rationis lumen, quo in suis actibus dirigatur ad finem.—*De Reg. Prin.*, Lib. I, cap. 1.

satisfaction of even his basic material needs.[13]   Moreover,
the fact of human interdependence in material things is
readily seen when it is realized that nature provides very
few ready-made goods for human consumption and that any
form of production, beyond the most elementary, requires
cooperation among men.[14]

It would be superfluous to labor this point any further;
in our present era of industrial civilization the fact of human economic interdependence is only too apparent. The
scope of human economic interdependence has expanded
with the extension of our modern industrial civilization until
it has become world-wide.   The limits of human material
interdependence are no longer confined to the boundaries of
the city-state, as in the time of Aristotle, or the provincial
state of St. Thomas' time; yet the extension of this interdependence beyond the confines of the state to practically
the whole world is but the natural development of the basic
social inclination in man postulated by both Aristotle and
St. Thomas.

The intellectual interdependence of men is likewise a fact
of common experience, for it is this which underlies our
whole system of education.   Man is dependent upon his fellowmen for the acquisition of knowledge.[15]   Thomistic
psychology rejects completely the Platonic notion of innate
ideas; while the soul possesses intrinsically the powers to
acquire knowledge, yet this knowledge itself comes ultimately from experience, whether personal and individual experience, or the experiences of other men.[16] If man had to
rely solely on his own personal experienices, the intellectual

[13] Classical statements of this fact may be found in Aristotle's
Politics, Book I, chapter 2, and in St. Thomas' *De Regimine Principum*,
Lib. I, cap. 1.

[14] *Contra Gentiles*, III, cap. 85.

[15] Here is meant knowledge of the natural order. But even in the
supernatural order, while divine truths have been revealed directly
by God to certain persons, knowledge of divine things is normally
communicated through the ordinary channels of instruction. cf. St.
Paul, *Epistle to the Romans*, X, 14-17.

[16] *Summa Theol.*, I, q. 84, a. 6.

development of the individual would be extremely limited, and the cultural progress of mankind would be impossible. Each human being would constitute a closed intellectual circuit. Progress in knowledge, at least in the natural order, can be postulated only on the principle of the intellectual interdependence of mankind.[17] It is precisely for the purpose of communicating knowledge that nature, which does nothing in vain, has given man the distinctive faculty of articulate speech.[18] As the circle of human society and civilization expands, the reservoir of human knowledge and culture increases. Modern inventions have greatly facilitated the acquisition and distribution of this fund of knowledge over the entire world. Thus becomes ever clearer the fundamental fact of the intellectual interdependence of mankind.

As a corollary to the preceding, must be mentioned the moral interdependence of men. This too is implied in the very notion of education, for any genuine system of education must aim, not solely at intellectual development, but also at the development of the will through the acquisition and perfection of the moral virtues. For true moral development guidance, care, admonition, correction, and example are necessary, all of which are an indication of man's moral dependence upon his fellowmen.[19] Even in the case of the hermit who lives alone, apart from the society of other men, St. Thomas recognizes the fact that before he could even attempt such a life, he had to receive the necessary preparation through instruction and moral training

[17] Non est autem possibile quod unus homo ad omnia hujusmodi per suam rationem pertingat. Est igitur necessarium homini quod in multitudine vivat, ut unus ab alio adjuvetur, et diversi diversis inveniendis per rationem occuparentur, puta, unus in medicina, alius in hoc, alius in alio.—*De Reg. Prin.*, Lib. I, cap. 1.

[18] *De Reg. Prin.*, Lib. I, cap. 1; *In Libros Politicorum Expositio*, Lib. I, cap. 1.

[19] The necessity of grace in the supernatural order is, of course, admitted. The things mentioned here are the normal means, even in the supernatural order, as secondary instruments, of moral development.

from his fellowmen.[20]   The case of the anchorite is
no exception of the law of human sociability, but rather is
an indication of its fundamental necessity; solitary life is
proper only for those who have already reached the state of
perfection, whereas for the acquisition of perfection in the
moral virtues life in the society of others is necessary.[21]

The interdependence of mankind in things material, intellectual, and moral gives evidence of the fact that social
life is a primary and immediate demand of man's nature.
Social life is not only natural, inasmuch as it is the expression of certain tendencies in human nature itself, but
is also necessary. For man is conscious of a destiny, an
end; for the achievement of this end it is necessary that
men live and develop in society.

II. SOCIETY

According to St. Thomas, a society is a group of human
beings united for the purpose of performing a common function or achieving a certain end.[22] This is society taken in its
most comprehensive sense. The two principal elements of
any and every society are significant in the definition given
by St. Thomas: 1. the constituents of every society, human beings, and 2. the end or purpose to be achieved. Since
the constituent element is the same in every human society,
namely, human beings, one society must be distinguished

---

[20] *In Pol.*, Lib. I, cap. 2.

[21] Et ideo vita socialis necessaria est ad exercitium perfectionis.
Solitudo autem competit jam perfectis.... In the preceding lines St.
Thomas gives his reason for this statement, which, at the same time,
is an excellent summary of the necessity of intellectual and moral
instruction: Ad exercitium autem hujusmodi juvatur homo ex aliorum societate dupliciter: uno modo quantum ad intellectum, ut in-
struatur in his quae sunt contemplanda.... Secundo quantum ad
affectum, ut scilicet noxiae affectiones hominis reprimantur exemplo
et correctione aliorum.—*Summa Theol.*, II, II, q. 188, a. 8.

[22] Est enim societas, ut dictum est, adunatio hominum ad aliquid
unum perficiendum.—*Contra Impugnantes Dei Cultum et Religionem*,
cap. 3.

from another by its end or purpose.[23] It is thus on the basis
of the end to be achieved that St. Thomas distinguishes
between public and private, temporary and permanent
societies. If the end to be attained concerns many men, the
society is public; if only a few, it is private. Again, if the
end can be achieved in a short period of time, the society is
temporary; if this involves a long period, or a lifetime,
the society is considered permanent. The family and the
state are St. Thomas' examples of permanent societies, private and public respectively; business groups are examples
of temporary societies, either private or public, depending
on the number of persons involved.[24] It is likewise on the
basis of end that St. Thomas distinguishes between the
supernatural society of the Church, which is concerned primarily with man's ultimate end, and the natural political
society, which is concerned principally with man's immediate end on earth.[25]

The objective, teleological character of St. Thomas' concept and analysis of society is at once apparent. Society
is defined in terms of end or purpose. Societies are distinguished according to their ends. Likewise, societies are to
be evaluated in terms of their ends, for the principal basis
for the evaluation of any object is its end or purpose.[26] Thus
St. Thomas lays the foundation for his hierarchical order of
societies, each society receiving its proper position in relation to the whole and in relation to other societies according
to the end or purpose it is expected to fulfill.

Human society, therefore, is not unique, but takes on
many forms, depending upon the object to be achieved.
Upon the hierarchy of ends to be attained by men, mediate,

[23] Secundum diversa ad quae perficienda societas ordinatur, oportet
societates distingui.—*Ibid.*, cap. 3.

[24] *Ibid.*, cap. 3.

[25] *De Reg. Prin.*, Lib. I, cap. 14.

[26] Secundum diversa ad quae perficienda societas ordinatur, oportet
societates distingui, et de eis judicari, cum judicium uniuscujusque
rei praecipue sumatur ex fine.—*Contra Impugnantes Dei Cultum et
Religionem*, cap. 3.

immediate, or ultimate, is established a hierarchy of societies. Of these, the family is considered as the primary society, both in time and in nature, for it is through the family that human beings are begotten, nourished, and supplied with the most intimate and immediate necessities of life. The family is a distinct society because it has a specific function to perform and creates definite relations among its members, namely, between husband and wife, between parents and children, and by extension, between master and servant.[27] The family is furthermore a permanent society, because of the lasting nature of the ties which bind its members together.[28]

But the family of itself is able to provide only the very basic necessities of life. There remain many needs which can be satisfied only by the clustering of families into a community or village, which facilitates trade and the exchange of goods. The village too has its limitations; only the conjunction of many families and villages into a larger and higher society can provide a complete sufficiency for life. What is this society? St. Thomas says that it is the "city" (*civitas*—to be taken evidently in the sense of the Greek city-state), which he calls a perfect community insofar as it is capable of providing all the necessities of life for its members.[29] This is as far as Aristotle would have gone; for him the city-state was the consummate unit of society.[30] St. Thomas, however, goes a step further and says that the

---

[27] *Summa Theol.*, II, II, q. 58, a. 7, ad 2 et 3.

[28] *Contra Impugnantes Dei Cultum et Religionem*, cap. 3.

[29] It is evident that St. Thomas is here speaking of the necessities of life in the natural order, primarily, physical, then intellectual and moral. These are the necessities for which the city or state is capable of making provision. For, in a later chapter of the same book from which this reference is taken (*De Regimine Principum*, cap. 14) St. Thomas shows that the supernatural needs of man can be adequately taken care of only by a supernatural society especially instituted by God for this purpose, namely, the Church, which is also a perfect society and of a higher order than the natural perfect society, inasmuch as the supernatural is superior to the natural.

[30] Aristotle, *Politics*, Book I, chapter 2, 1252b.

province (*provincia*) is a still more perfect community; to the provision of the necessities of life it adds the further good of greater protection and mutual aid against outside dangers. It will be helpful to see this passage in its entirety.

> Now, since men must live in a group, because they are not sufficient unto themselves to procure the necessities of life were they to remain solitary, it follows that a society will be the more perfect the more it is sufficient unto itself to procure the necessities of life. There is, indeed, to some extent sufficiency for life in one family of one household, namely in so far as pertains to the natural acts of nourishment and the begetting of offspring and other things of this kind; it exists, furthermore, in one village with regard to those things which belong to one trade; but it exists in a city [*civitas*], which is a perfect community, with regard to all the necessities of life; but still more in a province [*provincia*] because of the need of fighting together and of mutual help against enemies.[31]

Here we see a gradation of societies ranging from the primary unit, the family, up to the perfect community, the city or province, both terms being used designate civil or political society, or to use the more modern terminology, the state. (The city or *civitas* would evidently correspond more to the Greek notion of the city-state, or to the free city-republics of the Middle Ages, whilst the province or *provincia* refers more to the modern idea of a larger territorial or national state.) The gradation is made on the basis of

[31] Cum autem homini competat in multitudine vivere, quia sibi non sufficit ad necessaria vitae, și solitarius maneat, oportet quod tanto sit perfectior multitudinis societas, quanto magis per se sufficiens erit ad necessaria vitae. Habetur siquidem aliqua vitae sufficientia, in una familia domus unius, quantum scilicet ad naturales actus nutritionis, et prolis generandae, et aliorum hujusmodi; in uno autem vico, quantum ad ea quae ad unum artificium pertinent; in civitate vero, quae est perfecta communitas, quantum ad omnia necessaria vitae; sed adhuc magis in provincia una propter necessitatem compugnationis et mutui auxilii contra hostes.—*De Reg. Prin.*, Lib. I, cap. 1.

each society's capability of satisfying more or less perfectly the needs of man; thus each society has its own specific function to perform and end to fulfill. It should be noted that St. Thomas admits of degrees of perfection even in that society which he designates as the "perfect community," that is, political society. Its degree of perfection is proportionate to its ability to make provision for the fullest physical, mental, and moral development of its members. If, therefore, because of changed world conditions, provision for the complete development of man can no longer be made by the isolated, individual state, but only through the close cooperation of the state with many other states, thus forming a newer, higher, and more comprehensive type of society—a society of states—the existence and necessity of such a society would be the natural and logical conclusion from the very principles laid down by St. Thomas himself. Such conditions have actually developed since the time of St. Thomas. Our task, then, is to examine the social and political teaching of St. Thomas and of later Thomists to see whether a society of states is postulated by its basic principles. To accomplish this task, it will be necessary first of all to consider in more detail the nature of the state.

III. THE STATE

The key to the Thomistic teaching on the state, as of every other society, is the concept of finality. On the basis of ends are determined the nature of the state, its function, and the essential elements of its organization.

The nature of the state has already been indicated: it is an association of human beings, a society, that is public, permanent, natural, and perfect (in the sense explained above). The state is public and permanent in so far as it comprises a large group of people who are united by ties that continue to exist during and beyond the lifetime of the individual members. It is perfect in so far as it is capable of satisfying more or less completely all the needs of this group. Furthermore, the state is natural in as much as it is necessitated by and harmonizes with the natural inclinations and faculties of the men who compose it, not in the deterministic sense that it is forced upon man as a biological necessity, but rather in accordance with the nature and dignity of man as a rational creature; reason and free will play an indispensable part and are, under God, the efficient cause of the state.[32] The state is not simply an extension of the family; it differs from the family not merely in size, but in its specific nature.[33] Hence the state does not necessarily coincide either in origin or nature with a particular ethnical group, race, or nation, which to a certain extent may be characterized as the biological or cultural extension of the family. What distinguishes the state from these and from every other type of society is not the number of people who compose it, their origin, habitation, or common cultural heritage, but rather its specific end or purpose. It is this specific end or purpose which delineates the state, or political society, most clearly and differentiates it most sharply from all other social groups.

The end or purpose of the state can be considered from two points of view: extrinsically and intrinsically. The first considers the state in its proper position and relation to other things in the universal order of being; the second considers the purpose of the state in itself. Far from involving any contradiction, these two ends are complementary to one another; in the philosophy of St. Thomas the intrinsic end of the state is properly integrated with the extrinsic end, as the lower to the higher in the universal hierarchy of being.

Reference has already been made to the precise manner in which St. Thomas, combining the wisdom of the Greeks with the doctrines of Christianity, established the position of the state in the universal order of being, values, and ends. As St. Thomas says, "we must form the same judgment about the end of society as a whole as we do concerning the

[32] Schwer, Wilhelm, *Catholic Social Theory*, St. Louis: Herder, 1940, pp. 242-244.

[33] *Summa Theol.*, II, II, q. 58, a. 7, ad 2.

end of one man."[34]   Now since the end of man is two-fold,
immediate and ultimate, that society which is concerned
principally with the immediate end of man is of a lower
order than one whose primary concern is the ultimate end of
man, namely the Church.   The state's proper sphere and
function consists in helping man to achieve his immediate,
temporal end in life, although it should also assist indirectly
in the attainment of his ultimate end.   Hence, the state is
not the highest good or the final goal of human life.   Although the state ranks high in the hierarchy of values, its
task is nevertheless immediate and temporal, subordinated
to the ultimate end of man's existence.[35]

The intrinsic and immediate purpose of the state is to
assist its members in the attainment of their immediate
end in life, temporal well-being and happiness.   Since the
state exists, not merely for this or that individual, but for
all its members, it is the function of the state to provide for
the common welfare or the common good of all.   The common good is then the purpose of all the activities of the
state.   It may be defined as "the totality of material and
moral conditions which, in a natural and normal order per-
mit persons so willing to endeavor to attain to temporal
happiness, and the eternal happiness towards which this is
ordained."[36]   The common good is not merely the sum-total
of what is useful and necessary for each individual, anymore
than the state itself is simply a collection of isolated individuals;   just as the state is something different from the
individual, so also is the common good something specifically
different from the well-being of each individual.[37]   It is not

---

[34] Idem autem oportet esse judicium de fine totius multitudinis et
unius.—*De Reg. Prin.*, Lib. I, cap. 14.

[35] *Ibid.*, Lib. I, cap. 14.

[36] Delos, J. T., "Christian Principles and International Relations,"
in *International Relations from a Catholic Standpoint*, Dublin: Browne
and Nolan, 1932, p. 32.   (By permission of Stephen J. Brown, editor,
and Browne and Nolan, publishers.)

[37] Bonum commune civitatis et bonum singulare unius personae non
differunt solum secundum *multum et paucum*, sed secundum formalen
differentiam.   Alia enim est ratio boni communis et boni singularis,

the task of the state to provide each individual member directly with all things necessary for his well-being and complete development, but rather to create and preserve that "totality of material and moral conditions" which will enable all members alike to provide for their own well-being, either directly, or indirectly through such intermediate societies as the family, the proper function of which is to make such provision. Hence, the common good is not concerned directly with the well-being of one or other individual, but with the welfare of all as a totality; but at the same time such a totality is not to be conceived as something apart from the individual members, for by the very nature of things this common good must necessarily (if it is really the *common* good—*bonum commune*) redound to the well-being of each individual member. Thus there is a reciprocal relation between the common good of all and the private good of each individual, so much so that, as St. Thomas observes, the private good or well-being of the individual is impossible of realization without the common good, and, on the other hand, the common good itself cannot exist unless the individual members contribute to it by their own goodness. Consequently, within the state it is the proper and normal procedure to seek one's well-being through the common good, and whatever is contributed to the common good returns to the individual and increases his own personal well-being.[38] It is for this reason that within civil society goods and institutions do not have simply an individual value, but also a social value, for they all have a relation to the common good and are means of promoting that common good. St. Thomas expresses it thus: "As the life by which men live

---

sicut alia est ratio totius et partis.—*Summa Theol.*, II, II, q. 58, a. 7, ad 2.

[38] Ille qui quaerit bonum commune multitudinis, ex consequenti etiam quaerit bonum suum propter duo: primo quidem quia bonum proprium non potest esse sine bono communi vel familiae, vel civitatis, vel regni.... Secundo, quia cum homo sit pars domus vel civitatis, oportet quod homo consideret quid sit bonum ex hoc quod est prudens circa bonum multitudinis.—*Ibid.*, II, II, p. 47, a. 10, ad 2.

well here on earth is ordained as a means to the end of that blessed life which we hope for in heaven, so too whatever particular goods are procured by man's agency, whether wealth, or profits, or health, or eloquence, or learning are ordained to the end of the common good."[39] Since the common good looks to the well-being of all, rather than just to that of one individual, it is of a higher order and "more divine" than the good of one single man.[40] Thus the state, if it properly performs its functions and achieves its immediate and intrinsic purpose of providing for the common welfare of all, is a blessing for all its members and a help to each in his pursuit of happiness.

In order that the common good may be attained, it is necessary, first of all, that order prevail within the group forming the state. For the members of the state have relations one with another and with the totality which must be properly ordered to achieve the common good. Order implies the proper arrangement of parts within the whole.[41] In the absence of such order within the total group, each member would seek his own individual good with the result that the common good would be neglected and the political society itself would be dissolved. St. Thomas conceives the state as an organic whole analogous to the body of man or animal, which, without the proper ordering of its members, would disintegrate. He likewise compares it to the universe, in which all the heavenly bodies are regulated according to a definite order.[42] To bring out the necessity of order within the state, St. Thomas designates the state as a large number of men held together by some kind of order or organiza-

---

[39] Sicut autem ad vitam, quam in coelo speramus beatam ordinatur sicut ad finem vita qua hic homines bene vivunt; ita bonum multitudinis ordinantur sicut ad finem quaecumque particularia bona per hominem procurantur sive divitiae suae lucra, sive sanitas, sive facundia vel eruditio.—*De Reg. Prin.*, Lib. I, cap. 15.

[40] Bonum multorum commune divinius est quam bonum unius— *Summa Theol.*, II, II, q. 31, a. 3, ad 2.

[41] *Contra Gentiles*, III, cap. 71.

[42] *De Reg. Prin.*, Lib. I, cap. 1.

tion,[43] and again as a moral organism or moral person.[44]

For the attainment and preservation of order within the political body some regulative force is necessary. Unless the moral organism of the state is endowed with some principle to guide and direct the members toward their common end, each would go his own way and the organism would disintegrate, just as would the body of an animal if it did not have some vital force to coordinate all its members. This is the thought of St. Thomas:

> If, therefore, it is natural for man to live in the society of many, it is necessary that there exist among men some means by which the group may be governed. For where there are many men together, and each one is looking after his own interest, the group would be broken up and scattered unless there were also someone to take care of what appertains to the common weal. In like manner the body of a man, or any other animal, would disintegrate unless there were a general regulating force within the body which watches over the common good of all the members.[45]

This regulative principle in society is authority or public power. Because it is an essential element of society, without which society itself could not exist, it is just as natural as is society itself and has its origin ultimately in God. Contrary to the opinion held by many of his contemporaries and predecessors, St. Thomas expressly states that neither authority nor society are the result of original sin, for both

[43] Populus enim est multitudo hominum sub aliquo ordine comprehensorum—*Summa Theol.*, I, q. 31, a. 1, ad 2.

[44] In civilibus omnes homines qui sunt unius communitatis, reputantur quasi unum corpus, et tota communitas quasi unus homo.—*Ibid.*, I, II, q. 81, a. 1.

[45] Si ergo naturale est homini quod in societate multorum vivat, necesse est in hominibus esse per quod multitudo regatur. Multis enim existentibus hominibus et unoquoque id quod est sibi congruum providente, multitudo in diversa dispergeretur, nisi etiam esset aliquis de eo quod ad bonum multitudinis pertinet, curam habens sicut et corpus hominis et cujuslibet animalis defleret, nisi esset aliqua vis regitiva communis in corpore, quae ad bonum commune omnium membrorum intenderet.—*De Reg. Prin.*, Lib. I, cap. 1.

are based immediately on the nature of man as created by God. Such authority is not the dominion of a master over his slaves, but the coordination and direction of the activities of free agents by another free agent towards their common good.[46] Hence, authority is not an extrinsic power imposed by an outside force upon society, but is intrinsic to society and is derived from the same nature that society itself is, namely, the rational nature of man, endowed with intelligence and free will. Thus, political power resides primarily, under God, in the whole people who form the state—so St. Thomas seems to imply when he says that "to order anything to the comomn good belongs either to the whole people, or to someone who is the vicegerent of the whole people."[47] The teaching of St. Thomas on the necessity, nature, and origin of authority or political power has been well summarized by Schwer in his *Catholic Social Theory*.

> But this authority is not an outside power. It is demanded by the same will that desires and creates the state. Thus understood, a nation developed into a state is the original holder, based upon the natural law, of the power of the state. The state develops because the care for the common welfare, as the final cause, unites the people into a state, and the collation of authority makes the permanent existence of this state possible. The two processes take place in the same act and are derived from the group that forms the state.[48]

[46] Tunc vero dominatur aliquis alteri ut libero, quando dirigit ipsum ad proprium bonum ejus qui dirigitur, vel ad bonum commune; et tale dominium hominis ad hominem in statu innocentiae fuisset propter duo; primo quia homo naturaliter est animal sociale. Unde homines in statu innocentiae socialiter vixissent. Socialis autem vita multorum non posset nisi aliquis praesideret, qui ad bonum commune intenderet. Multi enim per se intendunt ad multa, unus vero ad unum. —*Summa Theol.*, I, q. 96, a. 4.

[47] Ordinare autem aliquid in bonum commune est vel totius multitudinis, vel alicuius gerentis vicem totius multitudinis.—*Ibid.*, I, II, q. 90, a. 3.

[48] Schwer, Wilhelm, *Catholic Social Theory*, St. Louis: Herder, 1940, p. 268.

In order that the common good may be achieved it is necessary that the political power or authority, which is inherent in the political body, be invested in one or more persons who have the specific function of directing the activities of all towards their common good. These persons constitute the government of the state. In the philosophy of St. Thomas government is not something subjective, dependent upon the will and whims of the ruler, but, like authority itself, is based objectively on the end of the state, the common good, for "the order of government, which is the order of a multitude under authority, is derived from its end,"[49] and "in every community, he who governs the community, cares first of all for the common good."[50] The form that the government takes, whether it be a rule of one man, of several men, or of many men, is of secondary importance, so long as its primary function and immediate end, the common good is attained. Governments are to be evaluated, not on their form or machinery of organization, but on their fulfillment of this end. This is the view of St. Thomas.

> If, therefore, a group of free men is governed by their ruler for the common good of the group, that government will be right and just, as is suitable to free men. If, however, the government is organized, not for the common good of the group but for the private interest of the ruler, it will be an unjust and perverted government.[51]

[49] Ordo gubernationis, qui est ordo multitudinis sub principatu existentis, attenditur per respectum ad finem.—*Summa Theol.*, I, q. 108, a. 4.

[50] ... in qualibet communitate ille qui regit communitatem, praecipue habet curam boni communis.—*Ibid.*, I, II, q. 21, a. 4.

[51] Si igitur liberorum multitudo a regente ad bonum commune multitudinis ordinetur, erit regimen rectum et justum, quale convenit liberis. Si vero non ad bonum commune multitudinis, sed ad bonum privatum regentis regimen ordinetur, erit regimen injustum atque perversum—*De Reg. Prin.*, Lib. I, cap. 1.—In regard to the forms of government, St. Thomas follows the Aristotelian classification of grouping them under two heads, good and bad governments, and subdividing each group according to the number of persons sharing the

Authority, the regulative force in civil society, is expressed through law, which is defined as "an ordinance of reason for the common good, made by him who has charge of the community, and promulgated."[52]   St. Thomas' notion of civil law, like that of authority, is thoroughly objective. There is no room for subjectivism in either.   Both are based on the social nature of man.   The precise determinations of law as well as of authority are derived from the principle of finality—the purpose of the state, the common good. "Therefore every law is ordained to the common good."[53] It is the common good, therefore, which determines the value of every civil law.   Since civil law is an ordinance of reason for the common good, its function is to adapt the general principles of the natural law to the particular circumstances of the community;   and since civil law thus consists of specific determinations of the natural law, it must be derived ultimately from the natural law and the eternal

---

highest authority, whether one, several, or many.   Thus the types of good government are respectively, monarchy, aristocracy, and polity, whilst their correlative bad forms are tyranny, oligarchy, and democracy, the latter form designating mob-rule, not democracy in its present meaning of popular representative government.   cf. Aristotle, *Politics*, Book III, chap. 7; St. Thomas, *In Libros Politicorum Expositio*, Lib. III, lect. 5-7; *Summa Theol.*, I, II, q. 95, a. 4.   In his *De Regimine Principum* and in several passages of the *Summa Theologica* (I, q. 103, a. 3; I, II, q. 105, a. 1, ad 2; II, II, q. 50, a. 1, ad 2) St. Thomas favors the kingdom, or the rule of one man, as the best form of government, whereas elsewhere (*Summa Theologica*, I, II, q. 105, a. 1.) he prefers a mixed form of government as the best, that is, a government composed of various elements taken from the kingdom, aristocracy, and popular rule.   There is no contradiction, however, in these statements, for, while St. Thomas recognizes the importance of popular participation in government, he also sees the necessity of "the rule of one" to insure the coordination of all organs of the government under a single head.

[52] "quaedam rationis ordinatio ad bonum commune, et ab eo qui curam communitatis habet, promulgata."—*Summa Theol.*, I, II, q. 90, a. 4.

[53] Et ideo omnis lex ad bonum commune ordinatur.—*Ibid.*, I, II, q. 90, a. 2.

law of God.[54] Law is one of the essential elements of civil society.[55] Consequently, while the state is characterized by a singleness of purpose or end, the common good, it is through the unity of authority, government, and law that this singleness of purpose is achieved, and through it one state is differentiated from another. "Thus we see that only those are regarded as forming one society [political] who are directed by the same laws and the same government, to live well."[56]

This brief outline of the teaching of St. Thomas regarding the nature, purpose, and essential elements of the state has indicated the chief characteristics of the Thomistic doctrine. The state is a natural society because it is based on the rational and social nature of man and is necessary for the complete development of that nature. As a public society the state embraces a large number of persons united by the bond of a common purpose, the promotion of their common welfare. Permanence is assured to this society through the stabilizing principles of authority and law. The perfection of this society is to be judged by its ability to provide adequately for the common good of its members. What is remarkable in the political system of St. Thomas is its thoroughly consistent objective and teleological character, its firm foundation on the nature of man and the principle of finality.[57]

But the examination of the principles of Thomistic political philosophy cannot stop at the isolated, individual state. The very notion of the common good involves relations with other societies outside the state. The more one state depends upon another for its complete provision

---

[54] *Ibid.*, I, II, q. 95, a. 4.

[55] Unde ad rationem populi pertinet ut communicatio hominum ad invicem justis praeceptis legis ordinetur.—*Ibid.*, I, II, q. 105, a. 2.

[56] ... sicut videmus eos solos sub una multitudine computari qui sub eisdem legibus et eodem regimine diriguntur ad bene vivendum.— *De Reg. Prin.*, Lib. I, cap. 14.

[57] Delos, J. T., *La société internationale et les principes du droit public*, Paris: A. Pedone, 1929, p. 192.

of that totality of material and moral conditions known as the common good, as is the case at the present time, the more evident becomes the necessity of the proper coordination of states through some form of society for the purpose of achieving a common good of a still higher order—the common good of all states and of all humanity, which will redound to the common good within each state, and finally to the well-being of each individual member. The principles of Thomism, when drawn to their logical conclusions, will lead to the concept of a society of states.

IV.   INTERNATIONAL SOCIETY OR SOCIETY OF STATES

While the principles of St. Thomas, if developed to their logical conclusions, lead to the notion and the necessity of an international society or society of states, it is not contended that St. Thomas himself explicitly elaborated such a doctrine. Nowhere in the writings of St. Thomas do we find an explicit theory of international society, as we do of society in general and of the state in particular. That St. Thomas did not develop a complete theory of international society in the modern sense of the term is not surprising; in fact, as Delos remarks, if St. Thomas had done so it would have been a pure anachronism, for at the time of St. Thomas the political organization of Europe was still dominated by the feudal system, and the formation of the new states along racial and cultural lines was still too embryonic for him to perceive their complete development into the national states of modern times.[58]   On the other hand, it was not so neces-

[58] Ce serait un pur anachronisme de demander à cette doctrine politique naissante des règles du droit public positif, ou même des principes capables de s'appliquer directement et immédiatement aux situations internationales actuelles. Née en plein régime féodal, elle n'avait pas à prévoir la formation des nations futures, ni la constitution des États nationaux modernes. Un Thomas d'Aquin, par exemple, pour ne parler que du plus représentatif des tenants de cette sociologie organique, ne pouvait deviner la nation moderne ni dans la Cité grecque qu'il avait sous les yeux en commentant Aristote, ni dans les républiques municipales de l'Italie dont il était originaire,

sary then to insist on the natural bond of mutual relationship between political communities as it is now, for at that
time there existed as a matter of fact (though also *de facto*
frequently disregarded) a bond of a higher order, namely,
the unity of religion, language, and culture within Christendom. But three centuries later, when the world picture had
changed radically, when the national states of Europe had
reached an advanced stage of development, and the problem
of the relations between these nation-states came into the
foreground, the political principles of St. Thomas were expanded and applied to international relations by a man who
is distinguished both as the originator of the Thomist revival in Spain and as a pioneer in the field of international
law and relations, Francis de Vitoria. Although an original
thinker and philosopher in his own right, Francis de Vitoria
remained faithful to the objective social principles of St.
Thomas. Like that of the Master, his whole social and
political philosophy is dominated by the notion of finality.
In his political system, too, it is the end or purpose, the common good, which determines the intrinsic structure of the
state, its internal public power, authority, sovereignty, and
law. After Vitoria had established the independence and
equality of the new national states and their inherent
natural power of self-direction towards the proper end, he
realized that these national states are connected within a
framework of law and mutual relations, of rights and obligations, so as to form a genuine community of states. Hence,
Vitoria visualized the state and the international society as
forming, one integral political order, the latter being the
logical continuation and development of the former.[59] The
accomplishment of Vitoria is two-fold: 1. he applied the
principles of St. Thomas to the concept of the new national,
sovereign, independent states; 2. he built a theory of international society on the basis of Thomistic social and political

---

ni dans l'État féodal du XIIIᵉ siècle, avec sa forme fédérale et hiér-
archique, et son système de vassalité.—*Ibid.*, p. 187.

[59] *Ibid.*, p. 201.

principles by preserving the thoroughly objective and teleological character of society, authority, and law.[60]   As a pioneer in the field of international relations, living at the very
beginning of the modern period, Vitoria could not be expected to have elaborated a complete and detailed doctrine
of international society, yet he did show the way.   His lead
will prove invaluable in the development of a Thomistic
theory of international society.

Before undertaking this development it is important to
have a precise notion of the terms used to designate that
society on which our attention will be focused.   In the
accepted usage of the present time we speak of an "international society" or a "society of nations."   Both of these
designations are of course acceptable if understood properly.
But to express with greater precision the concept of this
society as it is used in Thomistic political thought, the term
"society of states" is preferable.   The difference is derived
from the distinction between "nation" and "state," and the
significance which each of these terms has acquired in the
course of its development.   The term "nation," true to its
etymological derivation from the Latin verb *nasci*, still retains a biological or racial connotation.   Originally it was
used to designate a racial group, but later became more and
more identified with the notion of a political group.   Hayes
thus briefly summarizes this development.

> As derived from the Latin "natio" it [nation]
> meant birth or race and signified a tribe or social
> grouping based on real or fancied community of

[60] L'importance d'un Vitoria à l'aube des temps modernes vient de
ce que sa doctrine a su mettre le droit objectif et le droit subjectif
dans leur rapport normal.   Le mérite de son oeuvre est double.   D'une
part, il s'est élevé jusqu' à la conception de la nation, et lui appliquant
les conceptions politiques thomistes, il a fondé à la fois son indépen-
dance, sa souveraineté, et ses droits.   D'autre part, il est resté fidèle
à la théorie du droit à fondement objectif; et par là il a posé les
fondements d'une société internationale qui réunit les États nationaux
et une même communauté non pas contractuelle, mais organique, na-
turelle, institutionelle, soumise à un droit objectif et par consequént
authoritaire.—*Ibid.*, pp. 199-200.

blood and possessed presumably unity of language. Later it was used in certain mediaeval universities to designate a division of students for voting purposes according to their place of birth.... Since the seventeenth century "nation" has been employed by jurists and publicists to describe the population of a sovereign political state, regardless of any racial or linguistic unity, and this description still enjoys general sanction.[61]

The term "state," on the other hand, denotes the political society as such regardless of the racial origin of the people who compose it. Although the use of the term "state" to designate the political community is of comparatively recent origin, dating only to the sixteenth century when the Italian word *lo stato* was first used in this sense, yet the state itself or the political community has existed from the earliest times, and has been designated by various names, as the Greek πόλις and the Latin *civitas, res publica, imperium,* or *regnum.*[62] The distinction between the two terms is based on the underlying principle that is responsible for the grouping of large numbers of people: the nation is a grouping according to racial origin and denotes primarily the physical and cultural environment in which the members of the group develop; the state is a grouping for the purpose of achieving the common good of all the members, irrespective of origin, through the medium of a common authority and law. It is thus that Delos distinguishes between the two terms.

As we have so far studied it, the Nation appears less as a society than as a social milieu in which individuals are born and from which they derive what is necessary for their lives. The national milieu acts on the individual through the culture and the character it imparts to him.

What marks the State, as distinct from the nation, is the presence of an authority, a power of

---

[61] Hayes, Carlton J. H., *Essays on Nationalism,* New York: Macmillan, 1933, p. 4. (Reprinted by permission of the Macmillan Company, publishers.)

[62] Schwer, *op. cit.,* p. 237-238.

Law, which unifies the group, binding together by rules of Law individuals and sections.[63]

Although the two terms "nation" and "state" are distinct in their original meaning and their primary signification, there are many points of contact between them; the tendency of modern times has been to increase these points of contact and to fuse the two so thoroughly as to make them practically identical. This fusion is well expressed by the current term "national state." As a matter of historical record, many of the modern states have originated from national groups which have cut themselves off from outside domination and have established their own political power and autonomy. This phenomenon, of course, is by no means modern, though it has received much attention in modern times because of the tendency of states to develop along these lines. Historically, the earliest political communities did develop from racial or clan groups. Although St. Thomas recognized the national (racial and cultural) elements within the state,[64] yet his whole political teaching is concerned, not with national groups, but with states or political communities in the proper sense of the word. As we have already seen, St. Thomas built his doctrine of the state, not on the theory of a common blood, soil, language, or culture, but on man's social nature and on the purpose for which political society exists. If these principles of St. Thomas are extended to the relations between political communities, the subjects of these relations are not national groups as such, but states or political communities possessing unity of authority and law. To designate the society formed by these political communities, the term "society of states" is preferred to the term "society of nations" or "international society; the purpose of this designation is, consequently, to express precisely what is implied in the term, as well as to preserve the completely objective charac-

[63] Delos, J. T., "Christian Principles and International Relations" in *International Relations from a Catholic Standpoint*, p. 31.

[64] *Summa Theol.*, II, II, q. 101, a. 1.; *In Libros Sententiarum*, III, d. 33, q. 3, a. 4, q. 1, ad 2.

ter of Thomistic political teaching. But since the term "international society" has become standardized by current usage, it will be used frequently in the following pages for the sake of convenience, but always in the sense of a "society of states."

Having made these preliminary remarks, our present purpose is to show that the complete political order, which is built upon the Thomistic social principles outlined in the preceding part of this chapter, requires the existence, not only of individual states, but also a framework of mutual relations between these states, which in its unorganized form constitutes the natural society of states, and when organized by conscious human effort becomes a positive society of states. Our attention here will be focused on the natural society of states, the purpose being to show that the exigencies of human nature itself require such a society. Reasons for the existence and necessity of a society of states will be drawn from a two-fold source: 1. the fact that nature itself has provided the basis and pattern for such a society in the unity and solidarity of the human race; 2. the principle of human sociability and the organic structure of society require a society of states to complete the social hierarchy.

The fact of the unity and solidarity of the human race has been recognized since ancient times. The Stoics of Greece and Rome, however, were the first to make this fact the basis of political thinking through their philosophy of cosmopolitanism. Christianity shed new light upon the concept of human solidarity through its doctrines of Creation, Redemption, and the eternal destiny of man. Though not expressed in just so many words, the notion of the unity and solidarity of the human race was accepted by the Scholastics and underlies much of their philosophy, as will be seen shortly in the case of St. Thomas. It is significant that when the development of the science of international law and relations began in modern times under Thomistic auspices, in the person of Francis de Vitoria, the groundwork was laid by an appeal in the very first instance to the "natural society and fellowship" of the human race.[65]

The basic reasons for the unity and solidarity of the human race have been admirably summarized by Pope Pius XII in his recent encyclical letter, *Summi Pontificatus*. In a single, brief passage Pope Pius XII expresses the results of human thought and Christian revelation on the question of human solidarity; the fact of the unity and solidarity of mankind, founded upon the natural order, is confirmed and clarified by revelations of the supernatural order.

In the natural order, the fact of the unity of mankind is based upon: 1. the unity of man's origin; 2. the unity of human nature; 3. the unity of man's dwelling place on earth; 4. the unity of man's immediate end and mission in this world.[66] These reasons are in reality a condensation of the Thomistic teaching regarding the origin, nature, and end of man.

The unity of man's origin may be taken either in the sense of his ultimate origin from God, or of the immediate origin of the whole human race from common human ancestors. Both reasons are valid for the establishment of the fact of human solidarity. It is in the first sense that Pope Pius describes "the human race in the unity of one common origin in God."[67] For man, as every other created being,

[65] Vitoria, Francis de, *De Indis Noviter Inventis*, Sect. III, 386. All quotations and references are to the edition and translation of Vitoria's *Relectiones* contained in the Appendixes of *The Spanish Origin of International Law, Part I: Francisco de Vitoria and His Law of Nations*, by James Brown Scott, Publication of the Carnegie Endowment for International Peace, Division of International Law, Washington; published at Oxford: At the Clarendon Press, 1934. The number (386) refers to the marginal notation in the present text, which corresponds to the page numbers in the edition of Vitoria's *Relectiones Morales* published by Simon in 1696. (Direct quotations from the English translations of Vitoria's words and from Scott, James Brown, *The Spanish Origin of International Law, Part I: Francisco de Vitoria and His Law of Nations*, are reprinted by permission of the Carnegie Endowment for International Peace.)

[66] Pope Pius XII, Encyclical Letter *Summi Pontificatus*.   [67] *Ibid.*

owes his origin to God, who alone is Necessary and Sub-sistent Being.[68] Biologically, mankind is likewise a unit, a universal family descending from the same common an-cestors. The fact of the unity of the existing human race is confirmed by the investigations of modern anthropology. But while the conclusion of anthropology as to the unity of the present human race postulates a common origin for all men, yet this science is unable to discover the identity of the original progenitors of the human race. Light has been shed by revelation on the darkness that surrounds the origin of mankind on earth. Thus empirical science, philosophy, and revelation supplement one another in estab-lishing the fact of the common origin of mankind as a fun-damental basis for the unity and solidarity of the human race.

No less important than the unity of man's origin is the unity of his nature; the latter, in fact, is the immediate consequence of the former. As previously noted, man is an organic composite of matter and spirit, of body and soul. That all men possess essentially the same type of physical body has been empirically demonstrated by researches in comparative anatomy and anthropology. But the more im-portant spiritual element, the human soul—that precisely which makes man to be an *animal rationale,* a person, an intelligent and free agent—is also essentially the same in every man, each having fundamentally the identical spir-itual powers.[69] That men do differ, however, in the quality of their mental endowments is apparent to any observer, but these are only accidental differences of degree, not of kind. Researches in race psychology have revealed no es-sential differences in the mental endowments of various peoples; the accidental differences which do exist can be explained by factors of heredity and of physical and cultural environment. From the viewpoint of anthropology and psychology as well as of philosophy, the notion of an intel-

[68] *Summa Theol.,* I, q. 44, a. 1.
[69] *Ibid.,* I, q. 76, a. 2; I, q. 77, a. 2.

lectually superior race is a pure myth. What is of importance, therefore, is not the accidental difference that exists between one individual and another, or between one group and another, but rather the essential sameness of the spiritual principle in man, for it is upon this that the concept of the essential equality of mankind and the true notion of human liberty must be based.[70]

Thirdly, the fact that the human race has a common dwelling place, the earth, constitutes a further bond of unity. The fact itself is obvious enough, but its implications are worth consideration. For, when Pope Pius mentions the "unity of dwelling place, the earth," he immediately adds: "of whose resources all men can by natural right avail themselves, to sustain and develop life."[71] This is the important point: the earth was created by God as the habitation of the human race to minister to the needs of all men, not merely to particular individuals and groups. The resources of the earth constitute the unity of means in the natural order for man to achieve his immediate end in this world.

That there is a "unity of the immediate end and mission of man in the world" is evident from what has already been said regarding the Thomistic notion of the end of man and of society; the immediate end of man on earth consists in "living virtuously," which implies the proper development of his physical, mental, and moral potentialities, as the means to the attainment of his ultimate end, the possession of God.[72]

To the natural reasons for the unity and solidarity of the human race Pope Pius adds those that are derived from supernatural sources: the unity of the supernatural end of man and of the means to achieve that end; the unity of man's Creation in the image of God and of his Redemption through Jesus Christ; the unity of mutual love and charity flowing from mankind's common Redemption and destiny.

[70] St. Thomas, *In Libros Sententiarum*, II, d. 44, q. 1, a. 3, ad 1.
[71] Pope Pius XII, Encyclical Letter *Summi Pontificatus*.
[72] *De Reg. Prin.*, Lib. I, cap. 14.

"These," concludes Pope Pius, "are supernatural truths which form a solid basis and the strongest possible bond of union."[73] Although these supernatural truths cannot be known by human reason alone, since they are beyond the natural order of things, yet they are very important for a complete view of the factors which make for the unity and solidarity of mankind. The powerful influence which these supernatural truths exerted in mediaeval Christendom and still exert on the unification of the various elements within the human race constitutes a sociological fact which must be taken into consideration.

Immediately after enumerating the various reasons for the unity of the human race, Pope Pius adds a profound statement which reveals the far-reaching implications of the fact of human solidarity: "In the light of this unity of all mankind, which exists in law and in fact, individuals do not feel themselves isolated units, like grains of sand, but united by the very force of their nature and by their internal destiny, into an organic, harmonious mutual relationship which varies with the changing of times."[74] The fact of the unity of mankind, therefore, coupled with the principle of human sociability and the organic structure of society, will yield but one conclusion: that there exists in nature, potentially at least, a society which embraces all mankind, which by the laws of natural development and through human efforts should be actualized in the form of an organized society.

The fact of the unity and solidarity of mankind, based as it is on the nature of man, implies the principle of human sociability. For, as has been previously shown, man is not only an intellectual and free agent, not only a rational being, but also a social being, and from his nature as a rational and social being there immediately springs a complex system of reciprocal relations, of mutual rights and obligations between man and man. The necessity of these mutual rela-

[73] Pope Pius XII, Encyclical Letter *Summi Pontificatus.*
[74] *Ibid.*

tions for the proper physical, mental, and moral development of man has also been indicated.

The principle of human sociability postulates the necessity of the family, social, cultural, and occupational groups, and the state for the satisfaction of human needs. But human needs do not stop at the frontiers of states. Especially in our present expanding material civilization the needs of man tend to transcend more and more the boundaries of states. If a state in which a man happens "by accident of birth" to live is small and limited in resources, it does not follow that the needs of such a man are also thereby limited, but only that the satisfaction of these needs will be limited unless the state is able to make provision for fuller satisfaction of these needs through relations with other states. Should the state refuse to do this it would be defeating its own purpose; it would be a contradiction in terms for a state, the very purpose of which is to make complete provision for the needs of its members, to set up barriers to the satisfaction of legitimate human needs. If the principle is sound that the state exists for the well-being of its members, then the conclusion is likewise sound that the state should reach beyond its own confines to other states to give and to receive mutual assistance, in order thereby to provide more completely for the common welfare. For "the 'full good of human life' which the state must give to its members cannot even be thought of apart from a wide sharing in the material and spiritual life of the whole world, as well as in the varied resources which the Creator has scattered all over the globe."[75] Hence, "it is evident that the same law of sociability which leads individuals to seek in mutual help the necessary support of their own weakness and native indigence, obliges States to obtain by close and constant collaboration the means of fulfilling adequately their purpose in regard to their own subjects."[76] And con-

[75] *A Code of International Ethics*, Oxford: The Catholic Social Guild, 1940, p. 12.
[76] *Ibid.*, pp. 14-15.

sequently, "the bonds which spontaneously unite State to State are more than a passing phase; they correspond to an essential need of social life, and in consequence find their justification in human nature itself."[77]

It is of interest to note that the Thomistic pioneer in the field of international relations, Francis de Vitoria, bases his theory of international society and relations on this principle of human sociability; these relations must be grounded on the "natural society and fellowship" of mankind. Thus, he makes the principle of "human society and fellowship" the first and most important title for the acquisition of possessions in the New World by the Spaniards. (In the mind of this impartial and objective writer the case of the Spaniards is only the exemplification of a general truth.) For it is on this principle that "the Spaniards have a right to travel into the lands in question and to sojourn there, provided they do no harm to the natives, and the natives may not prevent them."[78] It is likewise because of this principle that "the Spaniards may lawfully carry on trade among the native Indians, so long as they do no harm to their country, as, for instance, by importing thither wares which the natives lack and by exporting thence either gold or silver or other wares of which the natives have abundance."[79] This is a significant statement by a sixteenth century writer on the philosophical principle underlying international trade. But Vitoria goes still further and upon this same principle grounds the right of all peoples to share in the raw materials and resources of the earth.

> If there are among the Indians any things which are treated as common both to citizens and to strangers, the Indians may not prevent the Spaniards from a communication and participation in them. If, for example, other foreigners are allowed to dig for gold in the land of the community or in rivers, or to fish for pearls in the sea or in a river, the natives cannot prevent the Spaniards from do-

[77] *Ibid.*, p. 15.
[78] Vitoria, *De Indis Noviter Inventis*, Sec. III, 386.
[79] *Ibid.*, Sec. III, 389.

ing this, but they have the same right to do it as others have, so long as the citizens and indigenous population are not hurt thereby.[80]

It would be outside the scope of our present plan of development to consider in detail these points of international trade and freedom of access to raw materials. These passages have been quoted simply to illustrate Vitoria's own application of the principle of human sociability. Yet a brief digression may be permitted inasmuch as it indicates the advanced thinking of this sixteenth century Thomist. The passages just quoted from Vitoria acquire an air of modernity when compared with the recent statement of an international economist of the present day.

At all events, it seems certain that any organization of the world for peace must include at the very least the following:

    a. Reduction of the barriers to the flow of international trade.
    b. Access to raw materials of all sorts for all nations.
    c. Access to markets for all nations.[81]

Thus far the emphasis has been on material or economic interdependence, not merely between individuals, but also between states. But these material things are only instrumental and secondary to the higher mental and spiritual goods. These, rather than material possessions, constitute the true fund of human culture and civilization. If the material needs of modern man transcend the boundaries of states, much more so do his mental and spiritual needs. The progress that has been made in recent times in perfecting the means of intercommunication has greatly facilitated the propagation and acquisition of knowledge throughout the entire world. The interchange of ideas and experiences between men of all parts of the world bespeaks an inter-

80 *Ibid.*, Sect. III, 390.
81 Cole, Charles Woolsey, "International Economic Interdependence," in *International Conciliation*, Carnegie Endowment for International Peace, No. 369, April 1941, p. 244.

dependence between states of the intellectual order. Thus, no state can justly claim to make provision for the "full human life" of its citizens except through active collaboration with other states. Consequently, the same natural inclinations in man for full mental and moral development which require the assistance of the family, intermediate groups, and the state, lead naturally to a community of interests and intercommunication of ideas between the people of various states and to an active intellectual cooperation between these states.[82]

Whilst the identity of origin and destiny and the community of nature leads to the notion of the unity of mankind, and whilst the principle of human sociability, first revealed in the individual's relations with his close associates, leads logically to the fact of world-wide material, intellectual, and spiritual interdependence, the picture is not yet complete, for these relations between men assembled in states, that is, between state and state, must have an organic structure. It is only by conforming to the requirements of natural society that a society of states can exist at all. And it is only by the existence of such a society of states that the hierarchy of human societies can be completed.

The organic structure of society is fundamental in Thomistic social and political philosophy. Not only does St. Thomas indicate this by his analogy of society to the organism of man or lower animals,[83] but he also lays down the philosophical basis upon which the concept of the organic structure of society is built. Just as the physical organism is composed of many parts, the functions of which are ordered by one central regulative force, the vital principle or soul, for the good of the whole organism, so also society is composed of many individual members whose activities are also coordinated and directed by a central

---

[82] Taparelli D'Azeglio, *Essai théorique de droit naturel*, Liv. VI, chap. V, 1361, Paris: H. Casterman, 1857.

[83] *De Reg. Prin.*, Lib. I, cap. 1.

regulative force (authority) for the common good of the whole society. But since the members of society are intelligent and free beings or persons, society is obviously not a physical organism; rather, it is commonly designated as a moral organism. The important point to be emphasized— and it is this that gives society its organic structure—is the reciprocal character of the functions and relations of the members of society among themselves and between the members of society and the society as a whole. As St. Thomas expresses it:

> It must be observed that every individual member of a society is, in a fashion, a part and member of the whole society. Wherefore, any good or evil done to a member of society, redounds to the whole society.[84]

In other words, the members of society are not isolated individuals, but are united within a complex system of social relations, of rights and obligations, all of which react on society as a whole and indirectly on all the members of the society; it is for this reason that these social relations must be integrated through a central regulative authority for the good of the society as a whole and all its component members. It is this system of relations and their integration through authority which gives society its organic structure.

But not only are the individual human members of a society interrelated within that society so as to give it its organic structure, social groups also must be integrated with one another in a social hierarchy. Thus, families are coordinated into communities, these again into other communities, up to the more comprehensive society of the state. As St. Thomas expresses it, "an ordered multitude is part of another multitude, as the domestic multitude is part of the civil multitude."[85]

[84] Est autem considerandum quod unusquisque in aliqua societate vivens, est aliquo modo pars et membrum totius societatis. Quicumque ergo agit aliquid in bonum vel malum alicujus in societate existentis, hoc redundat in totam societatem.—*Summa Theol.*, I, II, q. 21, a. 3. English translation, vol. VI, p. 273.

[85] *Ibid.*, III, q. 8, a. 1, ad 2.

It was Vitoria again who carried this doctrine of St. Thomas regarding the organic structure of society to its logical conclusion and thus completed the hierarchy of social and political institutions. The individual state does not stand at the apex of the social hierarchy, for, as Vitoria perceived, individual states must be supplemented by the more comprehensive society of states. As the interdependence of state increases, the necessity of this society as the crown of the social structure becomes more and more apparent. In this society of states the members are not individual men as such, but men assembled in political societies; in other words, the members are sovereign and autonomous states. The society of states represents the extension of the principles of political society to the field of inter-state relations. As Delos observes, Vitoria was one of the first to perceive clearly the unity of the principles of public law, namely, that the same natural political principles are applicable analogously to the state, in its internal affairs, and to the society of states, or states in their external relations with one another, and that because of this identity of basic principles, the state and the society of states form an integral political order and a complete organic social hierarchy.[86]

Two passages may be quoted from the writings of Vitoria

[86] Mais Vitoria,—l'un des premiers auteurs qui aient traité de la société internationale,—a bien discerné ce que nous appellerions "l'unité" des principes du droit public. Non pas que le droit public interne, et le droit public internationale, ne soient pas deux disciplines juridiques distinctes; mais *l'État*, d'une part, et la *Société internationale*, d'autre part, sont deux formes naturelles de *Société politique*, qui, subordonnés, s'appellent l'une l'outre et se completent pour constituer l'ordre politique integral. Il y a donc des principes puiseś dans le nature même des sociétés politiques qui trouve une application analogue dans l'État et dans la Société internationale. S'il y a un ordre politique interne ou national, et un ordre politique international, l'un et l'autre sont dominés et commandés par des principes fondamentaux uniques, qui se vérifient dans l'une et dans l'autre société, et qui assurent l'unité de l'ordre politique.—Delos, *La société internationale et les principes du droit public*, p. 201.

which give evidence of the Spanish Thomist's grasp of this integral political order and its implications. In the first of these passages Vitoria is treating of international law and shows that it derives its binding force from an authority which transcends the state.

> From all that has been said, a corollary may be inferred, namely: that international law has not only the force of a pact or agreement among men, but also the force of a law; for the world as a whole, being in a way one single State, has the power to create laws that are just and fitting for all persons, as are the rules of international law. Consequently, it is clear that they who violate these international rules, whether in peace or in war, commit a mortal sin; moreover, in the gravest matters, such as the inviolability of ambassadors, it is not permissible for one country to refuse to be bound by international law, the matter having been established by the authority of the whole world.[87]

The context of the second passage deals with the criteria for a just war. To the criteria generally accepted by the Scholastics, Vitoria adds another: the common good of the world or society of states as a whole.

> Nay more, since one nation is a part of the whole world and since the Christian province is a part of the whole Christian State, if any war should be advantageous to one province or nation but injurious to the world or to Christendom, it is my belief that, for this very reason, that war is unjust.[88]

These are remarkable statements that anticipate by four centuries the efforts of The Hague and Geneva. What is worthy of note is not only their advanced and prophetic character, but also the fact that they are thoroughly consistent with the objective, organic concept of society which dominates Thomistic social and political thinking. Vitoria's total, integral, organic political order is the logical outgrowth of St. Thomas' basic political principles. As in-

[87] Vitoria, *De Potestate Civili*, 219.   [88] *Ibid.*, 203-204.

dividuals cannot live well in isolation, neither can states; as individuals need the assistance of others and enter into relations with one another, so also must states; as the product of these mutual relations among individuals is civil society, so also the mutual and necessary relations between states should produce a society of states; finally, just as the individual members of civil society are directed by a common authority, so also should the state-members of the society of states be coordinated by "the authority of the whole world." Thus, while there is a natural, unorganized community of peoples, based on the similarity of nature and needs of mankind, this community possesses potential power which must be actualized through human efforts, and thus developed into an organized society of states.

> This is Vitoria's view of an organized world. It is the view of many today whose ideal may be termed the organic conception of the international community which looks toward a federation of nations.[89]

It is the organic structure of the society of states which, according to Scott, distinguishes Vitoria's concept of the international community from that of the other great Spanish pioneer in the field of international law and relations, Francis Suarez. The society of states which Vitoria visualized is organic, that of Suarez is inorganic—a distinction which has come down to our own times.

> There was, however, an essential difference between the international community of Suárez and that of Victoria. To the former, the community of states was inorganic. It existed because the states existed and had need of relations, one with the other, of "mutual assistance, association and intercourse." But the community which he had in mind was not an organized community, with law-making and law-enforcing powers. The laws of the international community of Victoria were created be-

[89] Scott, James Brown, *Law, the State, and the International Community*, I, p. 322. (Reprinted by permission of Columbia University Press.)

cause the community had "the power to create"
them, just as it had the power, backed by the
authority of the world, to enforce them. The
international community of Suárez was governed
by laws introduced slowly, unconsciously, by custom, in his own words, "by the habitual conduct of
nations."

We of today are not infrequently pleased to consider ourselves as originators, specially in matters
international; but in point of fact the two great
modern conceptions of the international community
are the conceptions of Victoria and Suárez. The
one—the organized community—the statesmen of
the world had in mind when they developed the
vast and complicated machinery of Geneva. The
other—that of an inorganic community, a gradual
development growing out of the mere coexistence
of states—has found expression in the international machinery set up at The Hague. The choice
of the future lies between the two.[90]

The Thomistic international society is, therefore, the
organic society of states envisioned by Vitoria. Our next
steps will be to examine the basic requirements for such an
organic society of states—again under the leadership of St.
Thomas and Francis de Vitoria.

[90] Scott, James Brown, *The Catholic Conception of International
Law*, p. 484. (Reprinted by permission of Georgetown University
Press.)

CHAPTER III

BASIC REQUIREMENTS FOR AN ORGANIZED SOCIETY OF STATES

In the previous chapter we have seen that there exists in nature a universal society of mankind, founded upon the exigencies of man's rational and social nature, and that, in the light of Thomistic social principles, this universal society takes the form of an organic society of states. The organic nature and objective character of this society must be emphasized if it is to meet the demands of man's social nature; a mere complexus of unorganized interstate relations, or a merely artificial and contractual society based solely on pacts and agreements, revocable at will, are not sufficient for this purpose. This statement will be clarified in the present and succeeding chapters. While the external organization of the society of states postulated on Thomistic social principles must be brought about by human wills, yet it is not for this reason merely subjective and voluntaristic, for, as has been stated repeatedly, but cannot be insisted upon too much, such an organization is demanded by man's social nature and is in accordance with his rational aspirations, and has, therefore, an objective basis in nature itself. Our next step is to investigate the basic requirements for a society of states thus rationally organized. It should be noted at once that this does not mean that we shall attempt to outline the external form which such an organization is to take or to set up the machinery for its operation. The draughting of a constitution for a society of states and the elaboration of its technical machinery belong to the realm of political science, jurisprudence, and statesmanship. The proper realm of philosophy is that of principles. Consequently, the requirements to be developed here are universal principles necessary for, and applicable to, *any* genuine society of states, irrespective of the external form which it may take.

The first of these requirements is the clear recognition of the end of that society: its common good. Every society must have a distinct common good; the society of states is no exception. The relation between any society and its common good is clearly the relation of finality.[1] From this first requirement flow all the other requirements which are necessary for the attainment of the common good, namely, those which are necessary in the states themselves in their acts of organizing, developing, and preserving the universal society, and those which are demanded by the organized society of states itself for its existence and effective operation. Consequently, after analyzing the notion of the common good as the first requirement, we shall consider: 1. the subjective requirements necessary in the states as potential or actual members of society of states; 2. the objective requirements of the society of states considered in itself.

I.   THE UNIVERSAL COMMON GOOD

According to the Thomistic principle of finality, the formation of every society is motivated by a specific end or purpose: its common good. It is the end, therefore, or common good which differentiates one society from another.[2] Since there is a hierarchy of societies in the natural order, such as the family, city, state, and society of states, so also is there a hierarchy of common goods, for each society is differentiated and explained in terms of the special common good it is expected to attain; the common good to be achieved is the *raison d'être* of any society, its final cause and motivating force; in the formation of any society the common good is, as it were, the projection in advance of the

---

[1] La relation est claire entre les notions de société et de Bien commun: une relation de finalité. Le Bien commun est la fin de la société, et toute société a pour fin quelque Bien commun.—Michel, Suzanne, *La Notion Thomiste du Bien Commun*, Paris: J. Vrin, 1932, pp. 50-51.

[2] St. Thomas, *Contra Impugnantes Dei Cultum et Religionem*, cap. 3.

end to be achieved together with the most suitable means for attaining that end.[3]

As in the hierarchy of societies, one society is a part or member of a higher society, as the family is a part of the state, and the state, in turn, is a member of the society of states, the good of any society, considered as a part of another society, is a particular good in relation to the common good of the higher society. The good of any individual member of a society is a particular good. The common good of that society is not merely the sum total of the particular goods, nor an absolute reality resulting from and independent of the particular goods, but the integration and unification of all particular goods into a single, higher good.[4]

Applying this to our present problem, we note that each state, considered in itself has its own common good to attain as the immediate end of its existence, but when considered as a member of the society of states the common good of each state becomes a particular good in relation to the good of the whole society of states—the universal common good. Such a subordination of one good to another does not imply that the inferior in order is deficient or second-rate in nature; it indicates, rather, the proper integration of each in the hierarchy of societies and common goods. In the domestic order the common good of the family takes precedence over the particular good of the individual member; in the civil order the common good of the state takes pre-

[3] Hiérarchie des sociétés, hiérarchie des Biens communs: la deuxième explique la première. N'est-ce pas en effet le but à poursuivre qui crée la société? Et ce but n'est-il pas le Bien commun? La société ne se constitue pas sans raison, sans *cause*. ... La *cause* de la société c'est le but à atteindre, par consequent il est antérieur à la société elle-même.

De même que, dans la fondation, il y a en quelque sorte projection du but en avant, projection accompagnée ou suivre les moyens aptes à établir la fondation, de même, peut-on dire, il n'y a organisation de la société qu'en vue de la poursuite en commun d'une fin commune. Et ceci n'est pas seulement vrai des sociétés civiles, mais de toute société.—Michel, *op. cit.*, p. 25.

[4] *Ibid.*, pp. 30, 37, 39, 90.

cedence over the particular goods of individuals and families; in the universal order the common good of the society of states takes precedence over the good of the individual state. Although the good of the individual, of the family, and of the state is something noble and excellent considered in its own proper order, yet in each case the good of the next higher order is still more noble, or to use the term preferred by St. Thomas, is "more divine."[5]

The universal common good does not consist simply in the juxta-position or summation of the common goods of the various states, nor is it something independent of them; as is characteristic of the general notion of the common good, this universal common good consists in the integration of the common goods of all states and peoples, their unification and elevation to a single whole of a higher order, to which all states should contribute and which redounds to the well-being of the member states; this is merely the application on a higher and more comprehensive plane of the observation which St. Thomas makes in regard to the contribution of the individual citizen to the common good of the state and its return to him in terms of increased personal well-being[6]

What St. Thomas observed in regard to the individual and the common good of the state, Francis of Vitoria made the basis of his international teaching. For him the "good of the world"—*bonum orbis*—was of paramount importance, intimately bound up with the natural law and the law of nations. It was this notion of the universal common good of the whole world which inspired Vitoria's advanced doctrines on the questions of international communication, commerce, and access to the resources of the earth.[7] The influence of this notion of the universal common good on Vitoria's teaching can also be readily seen from the fact that he added it as one of the criteria for a just war.[8] In

[5] *Summa Theol.*, II, II, q. 31, a. 3, ad 2.
[6] *Ibid.*, II, II, q. 47, a. 10, ad 2.
[7] Vitoria, *De Indis*, Sect. III, 386-391.
[8] Vitoria, *De Potestate Civili*, 203-204.

the mind of Vitoria, this universal common good of the whole world exists prior to the formation of any organized universal society of states; as as matter of fact, it is the one great motivating force, the final cause, which must inspire the formation of such a society. For this universal common good is the natural and objective norm for the promotion of the general welfare of all peoples in accordance with the law of nature and the designs of the eternal Lawgiver and Creator of nature.[9]

In its more concrete form, as constituting the end of the society of states, Delos has described this universal common good which looks to the general welfare of all peoples, assembled in political communities, as "an ensemble of rules, institutions, relations, and organizations that facilitates and ensures a cooperation through which justice and peace in interstate relations are guaranteed."[10]

Two essential elements are implied in the notion of the universal common good: 1. the preservation of peace and order among states, 2. the promotion of the economic, social,

[9] Denn es gibt nach Vittoria ein bonum orbis, ein Gemeinwohl aller Völker, das nicht aus ihrem Willen hervorgeht und ebensowenig wie die natürliche Existenz und das natürliche Recht des einzelnen Staates nicht einmal durch die übereinkunft aller Staaten aufgehoben werden könnte, "nec orbis totius consensu tolli et abrogari possit." ... Das Gemeinwohl der ganze Welt ruht in der communitas naturalissimae communicationis, in dem ganz naturgegebenen Verkehr einer umfassenden Zivilization, einer natürlichen Arbeitsteilung der Völker, die kein positives Völkerrecht aufheben kann, weil die Natur selber sie den sterblichen suggeriert hat. Die Vorzüge eines ungehinderten Weltverkehrs, der die natürlichen Schätze der verschiedenen Völker zum Vorteil aller einzelnen Staaten zugänglich macht, begründen ein bonum orbis, ein objectives Gemeinwohl des internationalen Lebens, das genau so unaufhebbar über dem Gemeinwohl der autarchen Staaten steht wie die salus publica über der Interessen der einzelnen und Parteien.... Das bonum orbis aber ist die natürliche Norm zum Besten aller Völker, unwandelbar von der Natur und ihrem ewigen Gesetzgeber festgelegt. —Dempf, Alois, *Christliche Staatsphilosophie in Spanien,* Salzburg: Verlag Anton Pustet, 1937, pp. 19-20.

[10] Delos, "Christian Principles and International Relations" in *International Relations from a Catholic Standpoint,* p. 49.

and cultural progress of mankind through collective institutions.[11]

A prime requisite for the existence of any society is peace and order among its members. This is especially true of international society because of its unique character of being composed of members with such widely divergent and conflicting interests as have the national states of modern times. It is obvious that there can be no semblance of a universal common good or general welfare so long as a condition of conflict and warfare pervails.

Since the time of St. Augustine, peace has become synonymous with order. In his celebrated definition of peace, St. Augustine stated that "the peace of all things is the tranquillity of order," and described order as "the distribution which allots things equal and unequal, each to its own place."[12] Peace, therefore, is not simply something negative, not merely an armistice or cessation of hostilities, but is something positive: a state of concord and order. In commenting on the definition of peace given by St. Augustine, St. Thomas notes that "peace includes concord and adds something thereto," for the concord required for true peace is not that which is based on fear, threats, or domination, but a well-ordered concord arising from a spontaneous agreement of wills.[13] Consequently, peace is not simply a passive and negative attitude—a mere abstention from threats and violations of the rights of others— but is a positive and active operation conceived by St.

---

[11] Muller, A., "The Organization of International Society" in *The Foundations of International Order*, Oxford: Catholic Social Guild, 1938, p. 64.

[12] St. Augustine, *De Civitate Dei*, XIX, c. 13.

[13] Pax includit concordiam, et aliquid addit. Unde ubicumque est pax, ibi est concordia; non tamen ubicumque est concordia, ibi est pax, si nomen pacis proprie sumatur. Concordia enim proprie sumpta est ad alterum, inquantum scilicet diversorum cordium voluntates simul in unum consensum conveniunt. ... Unde concordia importat unionem appetituum diversorum appetentium; pax autem supra hanc unionem importat etiam appetituum unius appetentis unionem.—*Summa Theol.*, II, II, q. 29, a. 1, et ad 1.

Thomas as a "work" of justice and charity. Peace is indirectly the effect of justice inasmuch as justice removes the obstacles to peace, but it is directly the product of charity, for it is charity, good will, or benevolence which brings about that spontaneous, well-ordered, harmonious concordance of wills which characterizes true peace.[14]

This thought of St. Thomas has a special significance for peace between states, as was eloquently indicated by Pope Benedict XV in an encyclical letter issued shortly after the World War of 1914-1918:

> If almost everywhere the war has in a way come to an end, and several treaties of peace have been signed, nevertheless, the germs of the old bitterness remain and you know well, Venerable Brethren, that no peace can have consistency, no alliance can have strength, though elaborated in daily laborious conferences and solemnly sanctioned, if at the same time hatreds and enmities are not quenched by means of reconciliation based on mutual charity.[15]

This peace, which is the fruit of justice and charity, is the *ultima ratio* of that law which regulates the external relations between states.[16] In common parlance, international peace signifies a *modus vivendi* in which states respect one another's rights and refrain from violating them. But when used in the Thomistic sense, peace means much more; it implies order—the ordering of all states towards the universal common good. Hence, the true notion of peace itself contains implicitly the second element required for the universal common good, namely, the promotion of the economic,

[14] ... pax est opus justitiae indirecte, inquantum scilicet removet prohibens; sed est opus charitatis directe, quia secundum propriam rationem charitas pacem causat.—*Ibid.*, II, II, q. 29, a. 3, ad 3.

[15] Pope Benedict XV, Encyclical Letter *Pacem Dei Munus Pulcherrimum*, May 20, 1920.

[16] La paix—c'est-à-dire, suivant la définition de Saint Augustin, la "tranquillité de l'ordre"—c'est *l'ultima ratio* du droit international. —Renard, Georges, *La théorie de l'institution*, Paris: Recueil Sirey, 1930, premier volume, p. 214.

social, and cultural well-being of the peoples of the various states and of all mankind.

In civil society, the common good of the citizens cannot be reduced to a mere protection of basic rights, such as the *laissez-faire* economists attempted to do, for the very notion of the "common good" or "general welfare" implies a positive promotion of the good of the citizens as a whole by the state. Similarly, in international life it would be a fallacy to restrict the notion of the universal common good to peace in the sense of abstention from aggression; even such a peace would be hollow and empty—as the facts of history indicate—unless founded on a more generous spirit which promotes in a positive manner the economic, social, and cultural welfare of the people of *all* states, of humanity as a whole, through collective institutions. As the individual man cannot normally attain his proper development unless he lives in society and works for the common good, neither can the state properly fulfill its function towards its citizens unless it strives for that universal common good which redounds to the states and their citizens. Furthermore, just as citizens have a positive duty to contribute to the common good of the state, so also do individual states have the obligation of promoting the universal common good.

> We may say of the State what is rightly said of man: as man cannot isolate himself from society without renouncing his natural destiny, so also the state cannot renounce international relations without renouncing the mission it has towards its citizens. . . .

> The obligations of the states to international society are first moral obligations, binding the consciences of peoples and of governments. They must conform to the exigencies of the common international good, first because it is the condition necessary for the accomplishment of their own natural ideal, and, secondly, because being the good of all, it takes priority over the good of the individual, and may subordinate it to itself. The states must, therefore, not only abstain from any-

thing that might compromise the common good, but must work positively to promote it.[17]

Such is the notion of the universal common good which forms the end or purpose of the universal society of states: the peaceful ordering of all peoples and states to the general welfare of mankind. For the achievement of this end it is necessary that states in their relations with one another as members of this universal society meet certain basic requirements. It is to the consideration of these fundamental requirements that we must next devote our attention.

II. SUBJECTIVE REQUIREMENTS IN STATES CONSIDERED AS MEMBERS OF INTERNATIONAL SOCIETY.

A. AGREEMENT ON FUNDAMENTAL PRINCIPLES.

Before the organization of a society of states can even be attempted it is absolutely necessary, first of all, that the states themselves (which, of course, means the people of these states, particularly those responsible for their government) recognize and agree upon the fundamental principles which underlie the concept of universal society. Without such recognition and agreement upon sound common principles, any and all attempts to organize an effective society of states will prove futile. These common fundamental principles are at root moral principles. No matter how comprehensive or complex a human society may become, it cannot be forgotten that such a society is in the final analysis composed of human beings, and that the relations between human beings, whether they are individual persons, or individuals assembled and organized into political communities—moral persons—must be regulated by moral principles.

The laws governing relations between States must be moral laws: for States are moral personalities.

[17] Delos, "Christian Principles and International Relations," in *International Relations from a Catholic Standpoint*, pp. 48-49.

> There is, therefore, a body of morals that govern
> international politics; these are not to be left at
> the mercy or to the play of economic, military, or
> financial interests. States are made by men for
> their own well-being, to help them to achieve their
> destiny. And so all political life, national or inter-
> national, is subject to a moral standard, in har-
> mony with the natural ideal of human life.[18]

Thomistic social philosophy is absolutely consistent in its
insistence on the universal application of its basic moral
principles, universal in its extension to all persons and to
all phases of societal life, from the family to international
society. It was this conception of the universality of fundamental moral principles which inspired Vitoria, for example, to defend so strenuously the rights of the American
aborigines against the intolerant claims of the Spanish Con-
quistadores. It was likewise this truth which urged the
same Vitoria to pronounce in no uncertain terms that obedience to moral principles pertained to public as well as to
private life, and that the obligation to observe these principles was binding on public persons as well as private person, on states as well as individuals—and this at the very
time that Machiavelli was proclaiming the opposite doctrine.[19] The significance of this truth at the present time
is indicated in a recent publication of the Catholic Association for International Peace.

> The false separation of private and public
> morality has been the source of innumerable mis-
> guided ethical and political doctrines. For one
> thing it has misled some men into thinking that
> the moral character of an association of nations
> differs essentially from the morality of separate
> nations and of the individuals constituting the citi-
> zenship of these communities. A Christian ethics,
> on the contrary, affirms the universal and elemental
> oneness of moral principles. The common citizen,

[18] *Ibid.*, pp. 34-35.
[19] Vitoria, *De Potestate Civili*, 219.

prince, president, nation, and world society alike
are under the laws of God and of nature.[20]

If, instead of being inspired by a common agreement on
basic moral principles as the norm for international relations, states are guided by a positivistic or pragmatic out-
look, the effects on international life will be disastrous in
the future, as they have been in the past; instead of a
genuine concern for the universal common good, economic
advantage or "enlightened self-interest" becomes the sole
motivating force in the state's conduct of its external affairs.
The result is the "drift towards chaos" described by Pope
Pius XII in his recent Encyclical Letter *Summi Pontificatus.*

> The present age, by adding new errors to the
> doctrinal aberrations of the past, has pushed these
> to extremes which lead inevitably to a drift to-
> wards chaos. Before all else, it is certain that the
> radical and ultimate cause of the evils which We
> deplore in modern society is the denial and rejec-
> tion of a universal norm of morality as well for in-
> dividual and social life as for international re-
> lations.[21]

In the same document Pope Pius indicates the nature
of these fundamental principles upon which states must
agree if they are to build a permanent international structure, namely, the principles of the natural law and divine
positive law of God.

> Once the bitterness and the cruel strifes of the
> present have ceased, the new order of the world, of
> national and international life, must rest no longer
> on the quicksands of changeable and ephemeral
> standards, that depend only on the selfish interests
> of groups and individuals. No, they must rest on
> the unshakable foundation, on the solid rock of
> natural law and of Divine Revelation. There the
> human legislator must attain to that balance, that
> keen sense of moral responsibility, without which
> it is easy to mistake the boundary between the
> legitimate use and the abuse of power. Thus only

[20] *The World Society*, Washington: The Catholic Association for
International Peace, 1941, pp. 6-7.
[21] Pope Pius XII, Encyclical Letter *Summi Pontificatus.*

will his decisions have internal consistency, noble
dignity and religious sanction, and be immune
from selfishness and passions.[22]

No amount of detailed technical organization can possibly
substitute for this necessary agreement on fundamental
moral principles in the formation of an effective society of
states. "It does not suffice to group States into a Society,
and to endow the latter with well-devised machinery. It
will be a lifeless body so long as there is no agreement of
minds on the certain and immutable principles which must
govern international life, or union of wills in the fulfilment
of the same ideal of justice and charity."[23]

B.   BASIC MORAL VIRTUES: JUSTICE AND CHARITY.

The recognition and acceptance of certain fundamental
moral principles constitutes, as we have seen, the sole secure
norm for the regulation of interstate relations and the only
firm foundation for the erection of an effective society of
states. The common acceptance of these principles is the
first step, but not the last; the principles themselves must
be made operative through the moral virtues of justice and
charity.

Justice is the primary social virtue "whereby a man
renders to each one his due by a constant and perfect will."[24]
It is the function of justice to preserve a certain equality
in human relations—not a rigid mathematical equality by
which each must receive the same share, but a moral
equality by which each receives his due—through respect for the rights of others which are derived from nature and protected by law.[25] Consequently, justice is an
"other-regarding" virtue, having regard for the rights and
needs of others; in its primary and proper significance,
justice always looks to others, and only in a secondary sense

---

[22] *Ibid.*

[23] *A Code of International Ethics*, p. 112.

[24] Justitia est habitus secundum quem aliquis constanti et perpetua
voluntate jus suum unicuique tribuit.—*Summa Theol.*, II, II, q. 58, a. 1.

[25] *Ibid.*, II, II, q. 57, a. 1.

can it be said to pertain to self.[26] Justice comes into play with the simplest of human relations, the association of two persons, and extends to the most comprehensive and complex of human relations, even on a world-wide scale; justice is, therefore, the moral basis of the whole social order.[27]

St. Thomas distinguishes two types of justice: particular and general. The basis for this distinction is the object with which each type of justice is concerned: the object of particular justice is a particular good, while the object of general justice is the common good.[28] It is, therefore, within the framework of society that St. Thomas seeks a rational basis for distinguishing the virtue of justice. Society can be analyzed in terms of the whole and the parts or members. Those acts of justice which have as their object the particular good of some individual member of society are acts of particular justice; this particular good may be due to an individual member by reason of an obligation on the part of another individual member, or on the part of society as a whole; in the former case we have commutative justice, in the latter distributive justice—the two species of particular justice.[29] Those acts, on the other hand, which have as their object the common good of the whole society are acts of general justice, which include not only the acts which are performed exclusively for the common good, but all acts in so far as they are directed to the common good as their proper object.[30]

Although St. Thomas developed his doctrine of justice within the framework of civil society as he knew it in his time, the doctrine itself is universal in time and extent, and hence is applicable in all its aspects to that society which transcends civil society. For the society of states is likewise

---

[26] *Ibid.,* II, II, q. 58, a. 2.

[27] Dougherty, George V., *The Moral Basis of Social Order according to St. Thomas,* Washington: The Catholic University of America Press, 1941, chapter III.

[28] *Summa Theol.,* II, II, q. 58, a. 5 et 7.

[29] *Ibid.,* II, II, q. 61, a. 1.

[30] *Ibid.,* II, II, 58, a. 5 et 6.

an organic whole composed of members having relations
with one another analogous to those of members of civil society; the states are moral persons, assemblies of individual
persons organized as single units, and as such are regulated
in their relations with one another by the same moral virtue
of justice as are individuals.   Certainly there is an important distinction between the mutual relations of individuals and those of states; the former are of the private,
natural order, whereas the latter belong exclusively to the
public and political order.[31]   Yet these two sets of relations
are regulated by the same moral and social virtue of justice,
for there is but one complete and integral moral order, extending to public as well as to private relations.   Consequently, justice forms the moral basis of the international
social order as it does of every other phase of social order.

  Of the types of justice enumerated above and applied to
international life, obligations of commutative justice exist
irrespective of any organization of states into a positive
society, whereas the obligations of distributive and general
justice exist in the full sense of the terms only within a
specific society.   The qualifying phrase "in the full sense of
the terms" is important here for the following reason: it
is evident that once a positive society of states has been
organized, the activities of such a society must be regulated
by general and distributive justice, and the obligations imposed thereby on the society as a whole and its members
are given a specific form, just as within civil society, state
and members are bound by distributive and general justice
in accordance with the circumstances of the particular state
in question; yet, on the other hand, it must be remembered that in the concept of Vitoria, and of Thomist thought
generally, there actually exists, prior to any positive organization, a natural society of mankind which has as its
end the universal common good—*bonum totius orbis*—
which necessitates, at least to some extent, the existence
and operation of the virtue of general and distributive jus-

[31] Taparelli, *Essai théorique de droit naturel*, liv. VI, chap. V, 1358.

tice on a supra-national plane. Consequently, it may be said that in both phases of international society—the natural, unorganized universal society, and the positive, organized society of states—both these types of justice must exist and operate. The difference between them in the two cases is one of determination and specification; in the natural universal society the acts and obligations of general and distributive justice are determined by the general norms of natural law; in the positive, organized society of states these acts and obligations are explicitly determined and specified by the institutions, decisions, laws and regulations of the society.

In their direct relations with one another states are bound by commutative justice, just as are individuals, to render to each state what is due to it. Thus, on the basis of commutative justice states are obligated to observe their mutual pacts and agreements, so long as these have been freely and justly entered into by the parties concerned. But it would be a fallacy to restrict the mutual obligations of states merely to the keeping of pacts and agreements, although even this modest minimum would be welcomed as a beginning in the reconstruction of order out of the chaotic disorder of the present world. But this is far from sufficient. Peoples, just as individuals, have certain fundamental rights by nature which cannot in justice be disregarded and trampled upon by other peoples. It is again to the credit of Vitoria that he insisted so strenuously and repeatedly, notwithstanding the opposition of his own countrymen and sovereign, on this very principle and its universal application to barbarian as well as to civilized peoples. Overruling all specious arguments based on the Indians' supposed lack of intelligence and culture and their adherence to paganism, Vitoria demonstrated that the Indians of America were just as truly rational beings as were the Spaniards themselves and that their political communities possessed the same fundamental rights as did the kingdoms of Spain or France.[32]

[32] Vitoria, *De Indis*, sect. I.

Thus, as Vitoria enunciated so clearly four centuries ago, states have the obligation in strict justice to respect the natural rights of other states with regard to such basic concepts as territorial integrity, freedom of government, due honor, and that "material personality" which is necessary to insure the common welfare of the citizen.[33]

Since distributive justice is concerned with the proportionate distribution of the benefits of the common good among the individual members of society,[34] it is evident that this virtue has a special function to perform in international society in the proper distribution of the benefits of the universal common good to all peoples and states. How this virtue would operate in a positively organized society of states, with a definite authority and government, is easily understood by comparison with its operation already existing political societies, namely, in states. The operation of this virtue in unorganized universal society is more difficult to understand. However, when it is realized that the obligation of exercising the virtue of distributive justice rests not only in the ruler or those who form the governing body of society, but also all those who have any parcel of social authority and perform any function in distributing the common good, such as the leaders of industry, finance, communications, education, the case is somewhat simplified.[35] Since there exists a universal common good, as we have already noted, its benefits must be properly distributed, and since such a proportionate distribution will not take place automatically, the obligation to performing this task rests with those leaders who, by their power and influence, can control the resources, immaterial as well as material, of the world. But the difficulty in definitizing this obligation, while at the same time perceiving its necessity, is in itself an indication for the need of an organized society of states.

[33] Delos, "Christian Principles and International Relations," in *International Relations from a Catholic Standpoint*, pp. 35-36.

[34] *Summa Theol.*, II, II, q. 61, a. 1.

[35] Tonneau, J., *Bulletin Thomiste*, Vol. XII, July-Sept. 1935, pp. 498-499.

The rôle of general justice in international life is of paramount importance, although it has received but little consideration in a world which has too long regarded relations between states as those of isolated individuals. As explained previously, general justice is concerned with the common good as its proper object, not this or that particular good. St. Thomas designates this type of justice also by the term "legal justice," but this designation has been purposely avoided up to this point to obviate any misunderstanding. The term "legal" as used today has a narrow connotation and is restricted to positive civil law. But the "legal justice" of St. Thomas is not so restricted. St. Thomas, in fact, uses the term in several senses: legal justice is indeed that virtue which directs to the common good by means of the letter of the law (positive law), but it also directs according to the spirit of the law, according to principles of natural law; furthermore, this virtue includes not only acts which are performed explicitly and exclusively for the common good, but also all other acts in so far as they are referred to the common good.[36] It is in the latter sense that the term "general justice" is used here, namely, that special virtue which regulates all acts which are performed directly or indirectly for the common good. Thus understood, it includes acts of commutative and distributive justice in so far as they are referred to the common good. Because of its exclusively social nature (its special object being the social or common good) this virtue may also be designated as social justice. When applied to social life on the international plane, we may call it, for want of a more precise term, international social justice.

The existence of a universal common good necessitates the exercise of general or social justice, by which all things are properly ordered to the common good. As in the case of distributive justice, obligations of social justice exist to some extent even in the natural, unorganized international society, inasmuch as there is a natural and universal com-

---

[36] *Summa Theol.*, II, II, q. 58, a. 5 et 6; II, II, q. 120, a. 2, ad 1.

mon good of mankind which must be safeguarded and promoted. When states are incorporated into an organized society, however, the notion of the universal common good becomes crystallized and the obligations of promoting that common good become definitized.

> In this case a new situation is created for the member states, with new rights and duties. There is a real international society, a social body, and not merely persons or individuals privately related. What characterizes a society as a distinct body is the union of the members for a common end which is the centre of thought and effort; it is the existence of a common good to which all members are bound to contribute. The necessary means towards this common end become the law of the society, the rule of action of the members, who are now members of a body to which they owe obedience: social obligation has taken the place of independence and isolation. The rules of interindividual morality remain, but now there are added the duties of social and distributive justice.[37]

Consequently, states do not fulfill their full obligation of justice simply by the observance of pacts and the fundamental natural rights of other states; this is indeed a necessary minimum, but there still remains the more comprehensive obligation to contribute positively to the universal common good through the effective establishment and preservation of such institutions and organizations as are necessary for the promotion of this common good. In regard to the necessity of this international common good and the obligation of states to promote it, Delos writes again:

> All states benefit thereby; all of them, by their very nature, have need of it. All must have recourse to it; all are bound to contribute to and serve it. The common good constitutes, in the interstate society, a principle of order and obligation.[38]

[37] Delos, "Christian Principles and International Relations" in *International Relations from a Catholic Standpoint*, pp. 42-43.
[38] *Ibid.*, p. 49.

Although justice, particular and general, provides the moral basis for international social order, it does not stand alone; if it is to be effective, justice needs the support of charity, benevolence, or good will. To use the expressive phrase of Pope Pius XII, international relations "must be actuated by justice and crowned by charity."[39]

The rôle of charity in the preservation of a genuine and lasting peace among states has already been noted. We have seen that, according to St. Thomas, justice removes the obstacles to peace by rectifying injuries done or damage caused, but true peace, the ordered concord of wills, is in the final analysis the work of charity.[40] The same Doctor says elsewhere that without the mutual aid of friendship and charity, society itself could not exist.[41] There is, consequently, a universal law of charity in the natural order as well as in the supernatural order. (In the natural order it takes the form of benevolence and good will, love and friendship, based on the likeness of human nature. In the supernatural order, this natural love of man for man is elevated to a higher level; the ultimate motive is no longer only likeness in nature, but is God, the Creator and final end of that nature; the basis is therefore supernatural faith and hope.) This universal law of charity binds all states as well as individuals. As in the case of justice, the law of universal benevolence or charity involves a two-fold movement, according to which states are obliged to show good will and benevolence to other states taken separately, and towards the community of states as a whole.[42]

It is the function of charity to supplement, strengthen, and animate the work of justice. The fostering of a true spirit of benevolence, good will and charity among the various states and their citizens will give life and soul to their efforts for the promotion of justice and the common

[39] Pius XII, Encyclical Letter *Summi Pontificatus.*
[40] *summa Theol.*, II, II, q. 29, a. 3, ad 3.
[41] *Summa Contra Gentiles*, III, cap. 131.
[42] *A Code of International Ethics*, pp. 44-45.

good of all, whilst "forgetfulness of the law of universal charity—of that charity which alone can consolidate peace by extinguishing hatred and softening envies and dissensions—is the source of very grave evils for peaceful relations between nations."[43]

Relative to the necessity and function of charity in international society, the words of Delos are again apropos:

> It is not as fantastic as it might sometimes seem to consider international relations as really to be governed by charity. On the contrary, it is futile and utopian to imagine a real régime of international justice apart from the leavening and life-giving influence of charity. A spirit of mutual good will, understanding and sympathy is essential. Without it, even the clearest and most fundamental obligations in justice will be evaded, and the best guarantees useless. For justice is sterile and lifeless, unless charity give it life and vigour in the hearts of men.[44]

III.   OBJECTIVE REQUIREMENTS IN AN ORGANIZED SOCIETY OF STATES.

Up to this point we have considered the existence of the universal common good as the end of international society and the moral requirements that are necessary in states to achieve this end. Except by way of noting the special relations and obligations arising out of the positive organization of a society of states, the points that have been considered so far in regard to states in their relations with one another find their application in the natural, unorganized universal society as well as in the organized society of states. The requirements to be considered in this section, however, refer solely to the organized society of states. It is true, as will be shown below, that Vitoria conceived these requirements as existing even in the natural, unorganized universal society, at least to a certain extent. Vitoria's

---

[43] Pius XII, Encyclical Letter *Summi Pontificatus.*
[44] Delos, "Christian Principles and International Relations," in *International Relations from a Catholic Standpoint*, p. 39.

reasoning is clear enough; these requirements do exist
potentially in the natural society of mankind, but can be
given actual, concrete, and complete expression only in an
organized society. These requirements are the essential
constituents of the organized society of states, without
which it would be impossible for the society to function
effectively. These requirements are really reducible to the
one primary requisite: authority. Since, however, there
are several specific functions of authority, namely, judicial,
legislative, and coercive, we shall consider each of these
briefly under the following titles: judicial power, law,
sanctions.

A. AUTHORITY.

The necessity of authority in society is a conclusion which
St. Thomas deduces from the nature of man and of society
itself: "If, therefore, it is natural for man to live in the
society of many, it is necessary that there exist among men
some means by which the group may be governed."[45] A certain amount of authority is required in every society, in
which it is necessary to direct several or many members to
the one common good; this is true even of the smallest of
societies, the family. But among the societies of the natural
order, authority is found in its fullness only in political
society, for it is the specific function of such society to provide for the complete common good of man (again in the
natural order). Political society in this sense is not restricted to the state, but connotes the complete and integral
political order which includes the society of states as well
as the individual states. Public power or authority is,
therefore, an essential requisite, not only for the state, but
also for the society of states.

That the principle of authority, according to Thomistic
social thought, extends not only to the state, but also to that
society which is more comprehensive than the state and

[45] Si ergo naturale est homini quod in societate multorum vivat,
necesse est in hominibus esse per quod multitudo regatur.—*De Reg.
Prin.*, Lib. I, cap. 1.

has as its end the common good of all states and of all mankind, is apparent from the previously quoted statement of Francis de Vitoria, the foremost exponent of Thomism in the international field: "for the world as a whole, being in a way a single State, has the *power* to create laws that are just and fitting for all persons, as are the rules of international law ... it is not permissible for one country to refuse to be bound by international law, the latter having been established by the *authority* of the whole world."[46]

As noted above, St. Thomas deduced the necessity and nature of authority immediately from the notion of order and the common good in society. Vitoria followed the same line of reasoning as regards the public authority of the state;[47] but in establishing the necessity of a universal authority superior to that of the individual states he added a new approach, arguing inductively from the existence of certain principles commonly accepted by men and nations, which he called the rules of international law.

The very existence of such universally accepted rules implies, of course, at least some recognition of a universal common good and the necessity of some means to preserve order among peoples. But Vitoria's statement implies much more; it is tantamount to saying that these rules of international law cannot exist and can have no obligatory force unless there exists at the same time some authority to establish these laws. That Vitoria regarded these laws as obligatory in conscience is evident from his own words. But these laws do not derive their obligatory force immediately from the authority of God (ultimately, of course, all laws do) as do the primary precepts of the natural law, for Vitoria expressly states that these laws (the rules of international law) belong to the category of positive law, rather than natural law.[48] As Taparelli observes, all writers admit that the rules which make up international law are positive

---

[46] Vitoria, *De Potestate Civili*, 219.   (Italics mine).

[47] *Ibid.*, 190-191.

[48] Vitoria, *Commentary on St. Thomas' Summa Theologica*, II, II, q. 57, a. 3.

laws, but not all have perceived the necessary connection that exists between the two propostions, as did Vitoria: there exists a body of positive international law; therefore there must exist also an international authority.[49]

The necessity and existence of a special authority transcending the authority of the individual states is, therefore, a fundamental postulate of the great Thomistic internationalist, Francis de Vitoria. The next question to arise is naturally: in whom does this authority reside? Vitoria sees this authority—"the authority of the whole world"—resting in all peoples (organized in political communities) taken collectively. Just as Christian states have the right to set up a common ruler, so also all peoples—the whole human race—have the right by natural law to designate the subject in whom this "authority of the whole world" shall reside. The following passage from Taparelli is indicative of Vitoria 's position on this point, provided, however, that it is interpreted, not in a merely subjective and voluntaristic sense, but in the light of Vitoria's objective, organic concept of universal society.

> But in whom then is this international authority to reside? To answer that question let us restate the foundation upon which all International Law is based. The nations are independent societies, their association is in itself a perfectly voluntary association. Thus authority resides, as of right, in the common accord of the associated nations and it is for the members of the association to determine under what form this authority is to be exercised.[50]

[49] La première loi physiologique de l'être social ainsi formulée: l'autorité est le principe constitutif d'une société quelconque. La société internationale et etharchique doit donc posséder une autorité, elle doit être gouvernée, dirigée dans tout ce qui est nécessaire à son existence, à son perfectionnement, à la fin qu'elle se propose. Comment pourrait-il exister un *droit des gens*, c'est-à-dire, un corps de lois obligatoires pour toutes les nations, s'il n'y avait pas une véritable autorité qui pût établir ces lois?—Taparelli, *Essai théorique de droit naturel*, liv. VI, chap. V. 1364.

[50] *Ibid.*, Liv. VI, chap. V, 1366. English translation quoted from Eppstein, *The Catholic Tradition of the Law of Nations*, p. 301.

The concept of authority itself states nothing about the form in which it is expressed or the machinery of government through which it operates. As indicated in the passage just cited from Taparelli, the choice of the form under which the universal authority is to be exercised rests with the collectivity of states. The principle laid down by Pope Leo XIII regarding the form of government in civil society is just as applicable to international society: "The right to rule is not necessarily, however, bound up with any special mode of government. It may take this or that form, provided only that it be of a nature to insure the general welfare."[51]

The scope or extent of international authority is intimately bound up with the notion of the universal common good. Authority, wherever it exists, must be proportionate to the common good, for of necessity it must be sufficiently powerful to achieve its task of ordering to the common good. Authority, therefore, is not absolute, but proportionate to the particular end or function which it is expected to perform.[52] The authority of the society of states, therefore, must be proportionate to its specific function of promoting the universal common good, which consists of peace and order among states in their mutual relations and their positive cooperation in advancing the general culture of mankind. This authority, however, does not extend to the regulation of details within the individual states, which can be adequately taken care of by the states themselves. The extent, as well as the limitations, of the authority proper to the society of states will be considered more fully in the next chapter in discussing the relations between the individual states and the society of states. But here must be mentioned the essential characteristics which it is necessary for this authority to possess if it is to accomplish its task of promoting the universal common good. This task cannot be effectively performed unless the authority of the society of

[51] Pope Leo XIII, Encyclical Letter *Immortale Dei.*
[52] *A Code of International Ethics,* p. 131.

states has the power to judge and decide conflicts between states, the power to legislate for the common welfare, and also the power to enforce its decisions and regulations. In other words, the three essential requisites for an effective international authority are judicial, legislative, and coercive power. Such is the view of Vitoria, based upon his general conceptions of international law. Writing on Vitoria's concept of the act whereby the society of states is instituted, and of its implications, Eppstein adds the following comment:

> Yet the act of institution, according to Vitoria's conception of International Law in general, would be more than a mere contract; it would consist in making articulate, positive and actual, a potential tendency or requirement of nature, which had the force of Natural Law itself. And the authority—judicial, legislative, and executive—once constituted, would promulgate or originate judgments, laws and operations which, if consistent with the postulates of Natural Law and morality would, *ipso facto,* command obedience and co-operation.[53]

Such is the Thomistic concept of international authority. But, as Eppstein observes, it is not possible to point to any institution or organization of the past or present—the League of Nations of today, or the Holy Roman Empire of yesterday—which embodies perfectly this concept of authority.[54] While the modern world is far from the realization of this authority, yet there are certain existing institutions (existing, at least, at the outbreak of the present war) which do reflect this authority to some slight degree.

> How near and yet how far is the modern world from that ideal will appear from an unbiased and objective appreciation of existing international institutions.

> Already examples are not lacking of such institutions, which, within defined spheres, have begun

[53] Eppstein, *The Catholic Tradition of the Law of Nations,* p. 281.
[54] *Ibid.,* p. 277.

to acquire the independence of national influence;
the enduring character; the quality of superiority
whereby they can demand information, judge and
decide—which are the attributes of true authority.
Such are the Permanent Court of International
Justice and the Permanent Mandates Commission.
It is a commonplace of the history of the League
of Nations, that a permanent civil service has alone
assured continuity in its action; and that those
of its ventures which have achieved any measure of
success are, in all but a few cases, those for which
a permanent directing or supervisory body has
been in existence. But between an international
legislature duly appointed and apt to frame and
edict laws for the common good and a diplomatic
conference able only to adopt resolutions *ad refe-
rendum*, there is an abyss. The second—which is,
in the main, the form of the Assembly of the existing League of Nations—displays authority under
its most tenuous and elusive aspect.[55]

As a writer in a recent issue of *L'Esprit International*
has wisely observed, if the experiences of the past twenty
years have taught us anything at all, it is the insufficiency
of a purely judicial régime to regulate international difficulties, and that an international society which lacks
genuine legislative and coercive authority is powerless to
maintain peace and order.[56]

The necessity of judicial, legislative, and coercive power,
as three essential requisites for true international authority,
is thus not only deduced from the principles of social and
political philosophy, but is confirmed also by experience.
Each of these three requisites will be considered singly.

[55] *Ibid.*, p. 281.

[56] Mais si les expériences des vingt dernières années nous ont appris
une leçon, c'est celle de l'insuffisance d'une régime purement judiciare
de règlement des différends internationaux. Une fédération qui serait
privée de toute compétence législative, outre celle qu'elle tiendrait de
la volonté unanime de ses membres serait à coup sûr impuissante à
maintenir définitivement la paix entre eux.—Rappard, W. E., "Du
Fédéralisme international," *L'Esprit International*, no. 54, Jan. 1940,
p. 11.

B. JUDICIAL POWER.

Little need be said regarding the necessity of judicial power as an essential requisite for an adequate authority in the society of states. Before peace can be effectively secured it is necessary first of all that the obstacles of conflicting claims be removed and difficulties composed through the proper administration of justice. According to the view of Vitoria, and of Scholastics generally, in the absence of supreme judicial power, a world court, the rulers of states act in the capacity of judges whenever the rights of their countries have been violated, and in this capacity they may redress rights and punish wrongs.[57] But the truth of the axiom *"Nemo judex in sua causa"* has been long perceived by states themselves as regards their difficulties with other states; the recognition of this fact is attested by the history of international arbitration. Yet an important qualification must be made here. It is one thing for states to refer their difficulties to a higher tribunal as a matter of voluntary choice and at the same time to retain for themselves the privilege of accepting or rejecting the decision of this tribunal; it is quite another thing for states to be obliged to submit questions of international import to a supreme tribunal and to be bound by its decisions. While voluntary arbitration deserves every encouragement as a substitute for armed force, it cannot be said to meet the requirements of the authority necessary for an organized society of states, for it stands the test neither of the objective, organic concept of such a society, nor of the experience of the past decades. The judicial power requisite for an effective society of states implies the power of summoning states to its tribunal, of obligating states to submit their disputes to it, and of abiding by its decisions. In his letter "To the Leaders of the Belligerent Peoples" in 1917, Pope Benedict XV pointed out this fact, and events since that time have brought out the full import of his words: "In place of

[57] Vitoria, *De Jure Belli*, 430-434. cf. Scott, *The Spanish Origin of International Law, Part I: Francisco de Vitoria and his Law of Nations*, pp. 210-212.

armed force should be substituted the noble and peaceful institution of arbitration according to regulations to be made and penalties to be imposed upon any State which might refuse either to submit an international question to such a tribunal or to accept its decision."[58]

C. LAW.

The second requisite for an effective international authority is the power to legislate—to direct the activities of the members of the society of states to the universal common good by means of law. Such legislative enactments are positive laws in the strict sense. The relations between states in the organized society of states are not regulated, however, solely by positive enactments of the international legislative authority: underlying these enactments are the natural law, binding all men under all social conditions, and that body of law regulating interstate relations, called international law, which has been developed prior to the explicit organization of a society of states. Each of these needs some consideration.

According to the philosophy of St. Thomas Aquinas, the basis of all human law is the natural moral law, which is the expression of man's right reason directing his actions to his final end. "To the natural law," therefore, "belong those things to which a man is inclined naturally; and among these it is proper to man to be inclined to act according to reason."[59] Hence, by reason alone man is aware of certain general norms of conduct which prompt him to act in accordance with his nature as a rational being. And since man's rational nature reflects the wisdom and power of the Creator, "the natural law is nothing else than the rational creature's participation of the eternal law of God;"[60]

[58] Pope Benedict XV, *Letter "To the Leaders of the Belligerent Peoples,"* August 1, 1917.

[59] Ad legem naturae pertinent ea ad quae homo naturaliter inclinatur: inter quae homini proprium est ut inclinetur ad agendum secundum rationem.—*Summa Theol.*, I, II, q. 94, a. 4.

[60] Unde patet quod lex naturalis nihil aliud est quam participatio legis aeternae in rationali creatura.—*Ibid.*, I, II, q. 91, a. 2.

hence, the natural law is the eternal law of God "promulgated by the very fact that God instilled it into man's mind so as to be known by him naturally."[61] This natural law, therefore, because of its origin and nature, contains certain primary precepts which are known to all men and which are immutable;[62] it is from this natural law that every just human law is derived either by way of conclusion or particular determination, no matter how remote that conclusion or determination may be.[63] This natural moral law must form the basis of international law as of every other human law. International relations can never be satisfactorily regulated by the rule of force, for relations between states are ultimately human relations and must be regulated in accordance with the nature and dignity of man as a rational being. In view of the present chaotic condition of the world, the recent statement of Nicholas Murray Butler on this point is significant:

> Moral law is sovereign, and the government of no people can refuse to accept that sovereignty without invoking the animal in man and turning back to the rule of force. When nations are collectively organized as human beings are collectively organized, and when the sovereignty of moral principle can be not only taught but, if need be, enforced by collective action, then and then only will the present reactionary, destructive and really terrifying chaos be brought to an end.[64]

A special body of conclusions drawn from the precepts of the natural moral law by common agreement among men and nations constitute what has been called since early Roman times the *jus gentium*, or "law of nations." Some of

[61] Promulgatio legis naturae est ex hoc ipso quod Deus eam mentibus hominum inseruit naturaliter cognoscendam.—*Ibid.*, I, II, q. 90, a. 4, ad 1.

[62] *Ibid.*, I, II, q. 94, a. 4 et 5.

[63] *Ibid.*, I, II, q. 95, a. 2.

[64] Butler, Nicholas Murray, *The Everlasting Conflict*, An address delivered at the 185th Commencement of Columbia University, June 6, 1939.

these pertain to matters bearing on the relation of one people to another; these constitute the basic rules of international law. Thus understood, international law has been developed by common agreement among peoples prior to the organization of an explicit society of states and its designation of a legislative authority; these rules have been recognized, at least implicitly, and followed generally since ancient times, but it is only in comparatively recent times that they have received systematic treatment in the writings of such men as Vitoria, Suarez, Ayala, Gentilis, Pufendorf, and Grotius. In order to understand the nature and derivation of these rules of interntional law, also originally designated by the term *jus gentium* or "law of nations," it is necessary to consider them in the light of the development of the term *jus gentium* and its usage.

In a previous chapter (Chapter I) reference was made to the fact that the term *jus gentium* was used by the jurists of ancient Rome to designate the principles and rules of law which regulated the lives of foreigners living in Rome, in contradistinction to the *jus civile* which was the law proper only to Roman citizens. This *jus gentium* represented the basic laws and usages common to the various peoples in contact with Rome—the common denominator of the laws prevailing among the peoples within the orbit of the Roman world. Such is the view commonly held by historians of law, although there are wide differences of opinion regarding the precise nature of the development of the *jus gentium* among the Romans.[65] It must be noted that originally the *jus gentium* was a body of practical legal principles and usages derived empirically from prevailing non-Roman laws; it was only later that the *jus gentium* was given a pholosophical interpretation owing to the influence of Greek, especially Stoic, moral philosophy. Since these laws and usages were

[65] For these opinions see Scott, James Brown, *Law, the State, and the International Community*, I, pp. 137-142; Phillipson, Coleman, *The International Law and Custom of Ancient Greece and Rome*, I, pp. 67-99; Nettleship, Henry, "Ius Gentium," *The Journal of Philology*, vol. XIII, 1885, pp. 169-181.

common to all the peoples within the sphere of Roman influence they were interpreted as conclusions drawn by the general consensus of men acting according to right reason, and thus came to be identified with the natural law of the Greeks [66]—an identification which has resulted in no end of confusion. Because of this fusion of juridical and phisosophical concepts, it is necessary for the sake of clarity to distinguish between the *jus naturale* and *jus gentium* of the jurists and the *jus naturale* and *jus gentium* of the philosophers. According to the theory of the Roman jurists, the *jus naturale* designated that law by which creatures act in accordance with their natural inclinations, and hence is common to all animals; the *jus gentium,* on the contrary, is proper only to rational beings, for it is right reason applied to human relationships and manifested through a common consensus among all men.[67] The philosophers, on the other hand, generally restricted the term *jus naturale* to natural moral law, by which human conduct is regulated according to right reason; natural law in this sense is thus restricted to human beings and comprises those primary principles of human conduct which are known naturally by man's reason; the *jus gentium* comprises those conclusions from the natural law which are so closely related to it that they are derived from it universally by practically all men, as it were, by common consensus of opinion. But what is most significant for our present purpose is that the *jus gentium* of both the jurists and the philosophers of the Roman period was a "law of nations," not in the sense of international law, as a *jus inter gentes,* but in the sense of a "law common to the people of all nations," a *jus commune omnium gentium.* In the body of the *jus gentium* there

[66] Scott, *Law, the State, and the International Community,* I, p. 107.

[67] The following passage from the *Digest* of Justinian, quoting the *Institutes* of Ulpian, is indicative of the jurists' point of view: "The law of nations [*jus gentium*] is that used by the human race, and it is easy to understand that it differs from the natural law [*jus naturale*] for the reason that the latter is common to all animals, while the former only concerns men in their relations with one another."—*Digest,* I, i, 1, 4.

were indeed some principles and usages pertaining to relations between nations *as nations,* but by far the majority were concerned with individual persons within a nation in their relations with one another. But insofar as certain basic principles and practices governing relations between nations were contained in the general body of the *jus gentium* it may be said (and in this sense only) that modern international law is the outgrowth of the ancient *jus gentium,* or "law of nations."

The first one to interpret the *jus gentium,* or "law of nations," in the sense of international law seems to be St. Isidore of Seville, who wrote in the seventh century. Although he does not expressly restrict the meaning of *jus gentium,* yet all the examples which he gives concern relations between nations, or at least between the people of one nation and those of another.

> The law of nations comprises the seizing, building and fortifying of settlements: wars, captivities, servitudes, postliminies, treaties of peace, truces, the obligation to respect the inviolability of ambassadors, and the prohibition of intermarriage with foreigners. This is called the law of nations because nearly all nations observe it.[68]

Thus, as Carlton Hayes observes, St. Isidore "reserves the term *jus gentium* for what we should now describe as international law, so that here for the first time we find that term fairly translatable by 'law of nations.' All the remaining matter of the *jus gentium* of the Roman jurists, namely, the law common to all nations (*jus commune omnium nationum*), he incorporates in *jus naturale.*"[69]

[68] Jus gentium est sedium occupatio, aedificatio, munitio, bella, captivitates, servitutes, postliminia, foedera, paces, induciae, legatorum non violandorum religio, connubia inter alienigenos prohibita; et inde jus gentium, quod eo jure omnes fere gentes utuntur.—St. Isidore, *Etymologiarum Libri XX,* Lib. V, cap. VI. Migne, *Patres Latini,* vol. 82, col. 199-200—(English translation reprinted from Scott, *Law, the State, and the International Community,* II, p. 241, by permission of Columbia University Press.)

[69] Hayes, Carlton J. H., "Medieval Diplomacy" in Walsh, *History and Nature of International Relations,* p. 76.

Although St. Thomas Aquinas expressly quotes St. Isidore, he does not restrict the term *jus gentium* to matters dealing with relations between people of different nations, but uses it in its wider sense as the general law common to the people of all nations. To understand St. Thomas' use of the term *jus gentium*, as well as that of *jus naturale*, it is important to keep in mind the distinction between the concepts of the jurists and the philosophers, a distinction which St. Thomas himself carefully observed.[70] It is only in this way that the different usages of the terms in the various parts of the *Summa Theologica* (which on first sight seem contradictory) can be explained. In the *Secunda Secundae*, question 57, St. Thomas is considering rights in relation to justice and here uses *jus naturale* and *jus gentium* in the sense of the Roman jurists, whom he expressly quotes;[71] in the *Prima Secundae*, on the other hand, he is dealing with law in relation to human reason and in this passage uses the terms *lex naturalis* and *jus gentium* in the philosophical sense.[72] In his answer to an objection that there is no difference between the *jus naturale* and the *jus gentium*, St. Thomas reveals his position and at the same time throws considerable light on the whole question.

> The law of nations is indeed, in some way, natural to man, in so far as he is a reasonable being, because it is derived from the natural law by way of a conclusion that is not very remote from its premisses. Wherefore men easily agreed thereto. Nevertheless it is distinct from the natural law, especially from that natural law which is common to all animals.[73]

[70] Laversin, M. J., "Droit Naturel et Droit Positif d'après Saint Thomas," *Revue Thomiste*, vol. XVI, 1933, p. 46.

[71] *Summa Theol.*, II, II, q. 57, a. 3.

[72] *Ibid.*, I, II, q. 95, a. 4. cf. McDonald, Wm. J., *The Social Value of Property according to St. Thomas Aquinas*, Washington: The Catholic University of America Press, 1939, p. 87.

[73] Ad *primum* ergo dicendum, quod jus gentium est quidem aliquo modo naturale homini, secundum quod est rationalis, inquantum derivatur a lege naturali per modum conclusionis, quae non est multum remota a principiis, unde de facili in hujusmode homines consenserunt:

Consequently, the law of nations differs from the natural law as conclusions do from first principles, and it is in this manner that the philosophers understand the two terms; but it differs especially (*maxime*) from that natural law which is common to all animals (*ab eo quod est omnibus animalibus commune*), which, of course, is the *jus naturale* of the jurists.   But throughout his discussion of the law of nations (*jus gentium*), it is apparent that St. Thomas is using the term in its broad and comprehensive sense as a body of general conclusions derived from natural law by mankind universally, in virtue of the same rational nature, and regulating the social relationships between man and man, "without which men cannot live with one another."[74] Nowhere, however, do we find in St. Thomas these social relationships restricted to relations between social or national groups;   hence, St. Thomas nowhere uses the term "law of nations" (*jus gentium*) in the restricted sense of "international law" (*jus inter gentes*).

It remained for Francis of Vitoria to make a clear-cut distinction between the *jus gentium* as a norm for regulating the private social relationships between individuals, and the *jus gentium* as the norm for regulating public social relations between states or nations;   and it may be said that it was from this distinction by Vitoria that the modern science of international law was born.   It will prove advantageous to cite Vitoria's own words on this important point. In his commentary on the *Summa Theologica* of St. Thomas (II,II, q. 57, a. 3), Vitoria first deals with the relation of the *jus gentium* to natural law and to positive law, a difficulty which evidently still perplexed students in his day.

> Here there is a doubt under which law the *jus gentium* is contained: whether under positive law or under natural law. . . .

---

distinguitur tamen a lege naturali, maxime ab eo quod est omnibus animalibus commune.—*Summa Theol.*, I, II, q. 95, a. 4, ad 1. English translation, vol. VIII, p. 62.

[74] *Ibid.*, I, II, q. 95, a. 4.

I answer to this, and say first of all that the dispute concerns the name more than the thing, for it matters little whether one says this or that. I say secondly, that the Jurisconsults make the law of nations too extensive, and include too many things under it, because as appears in that title, *De Justitia et Jure*, they make the *jus gentium* extend to all those things in which brute animals do not participate—so that they make it extend to all those things which are common to man alone. But they call natural law only those things which are extended to all created things. And so, according to them, natural law is common to all animals, rational and irrational.... Therefore we say with St. Thomas that the natural law is an absolute good, and not a relative good: but the *jus gentium* is only relatively good, therefore it is said that the *jus gentium* has not equity of itself, from its own nature, but was established as inviolable, from agreement among men. And so I answer the principal doubt with this conclusion: That *jus gentium* ought to be placed more under positive law than under natural law. Whence the theologians do not posit those examples which the Jurisconsults posit, concerning the worship of God and the honouring of parents, but others: either concerning personal property, or other things which have not of themselves equity, that is to say of their own nature; such as the manumission of slaves, the propriety of possessions, the conservation of the kingdom, etc. The dispute is one of words, and therefore one may speak as a jurist or as a theologian, interpreting the terms loosely or closely—however one may consider they ought to be taken.[75]

[75] Vitoria, Francisco de, *De Jure Gentium et Naturali*, A Commentary on St. Thomas Aquinas, *Summa Theol.*, II, II, q. 57, a. 3. English translation used here is by Francis Crane Macken and is found as Appendix E in Scott, *The Spanish Origin of International Law, Part I: Francisco de Vitoria and his Law of Nations*, pp. CXI-CXIV. For original Latin text see: Francisco de Vitoria, O.P., *Comentarios a la Secunda Secundae de Santo Tomás*, Tomo III, "De Justitia," edited by R. P. Vicente Beltrán de Heredia, O.P., as volume IV of "Biblioteca de Teólogos Españoles," Salamanca, 1934.

Having disposed of this difficulty, Vitoria proceeds to what he considers a much more serious doubt, namely, the binding force of the *jus gentium;* it is in this connection that he makes the all-important distinction between the private and the public law of nations.

> But the greatest doubt is a moral one. If the *jus gentium* is of the positive law as has been said, and not of the natural law, is it a sin to violate the *jus gentium?* It is answered that, speaking of those things which are done in a legitimate manner according to the *jus gentium,* that is: concerning human written law there is no doubt but that to act contrary to it is a sin, because those laws, as we have said many times, are binding in the court of conscience. But there is a doubt whether it may be a sin to violate the *jus gentium* (to which some have not yet given their sanction), that is to say, to violate a law of nations which is unwritten, or even written, and which does not bind all men who are in the world. Let us make this clear by the case of the killing of an ambassador—which is contrary to the *jus gentium*—under circumstances where all are not obliged to observe the *jus gentium,* since the *jus gentium* may not be natural law as we have supposed. So let us imagine that we have a war with the French, and the French send an ambassador whom the Spaniards kill contrary to the *jus gentium.* How then are you to judge and know that we have not admitted that *jus gentium,* and that we have sinned in killing an enemy? To this, it is answered by the supposition that the *jus gentium* is twofold, just as positive law is twofold, as we have said above in article 2. There is one kind of positive law taken from private agreement and consensus, and another kind taken from public agreement. In like manner we say of the *jus gentium* that a certain kind of *jus gentium* is from the common consensus of all peoples and nations, and in that way ambassadors have come to be admitted under the *jus gentium,* and are inviolable among all nations. For the *jus gentium* so closely approaches to the natural law that the natural law cannot be preserved

without this *jus gentium*. And so of peace—by the law of nature, if wars should arise, it is the public business to bring about a peace by the sending of ambassadors. And otherwise, if ambassadors should not be admitted by the *jus gentium*, they could not put an end to wars.[76]

Here, then, we have the germ from which sprang the modern science of international law, developed by Vitoria himself in his *Relectio de Indis Noviter Inventis* and *Relectio de Jure Belli*, and expanded by such successors at Suarez, Gentili, Pufendorf, and particularly Grotius. Here we find Vitoria's conception of the *jus gentium* as true international law; here too we see his teaching regarding the nature, origin, and binding force of this international law. The two *Relectiones*, to which reference has just been made, indicate the scope of this international law and the applications which Vitoria made of his own principles to such important questions as discovery and colonization, freedom of travel, communication and trade, promotion of peace, and the conduct of war.[77] These are the elements of that international law, which, as Vitoria says, "has not only the force of a pact and agreement among men, but also the force of a law . . . having been established by the authority of the whole world."[78] The international law which we have been considering thus far is positive law to a certain extent, yet closely related to the natural moral law; it is based upon the natural law and derived positively from it by the common consensus and agreement of all nations—"the authority of the whole world;" it exists, therefore, and regulates

[76] *Ibid.*

[77] For a summary of the points of international law treated by Vitoria see Scott, J. B., *The Catholic Conception of International Law*, pp. 487-490; also Scott, J. B., *The Spanish Origin of International Law, Part I: Francisco de Vitoria and his Law of Nations*, pp. 283-288; for a summary of the principles of modern international law which are traceable to Vitoria, see Wright, Herbert, "International Law: Old Wine in New Bottles," *The Catholic World*, vol. CXXXII, no. 791, February 1931, pp. 513-521.

[78] Vitoria, *De Potestate Civili*, 219.

the relation between states prior to the organization of these states into an explicit society of states.

After the organization of the society of states and the institution of a legislative organ empowered with the authority of the society, the enactments of this legislative authority for the universal common good have the force of positive law in the strict sense of the term. As the positive civil laws of the state are particular determinations of the natural law,[79] so also these positive international laws will be particular determinations of the natural law, and of that "law of nations" which is derived from the natural law, to meet the exigencies of the universal common good according to the changing circumstances of time and the economic, political, social, and cultural conditions of the world. These positive international laws, established for the universal common good of humanity, will have a binding force, and as Delos points out, will obligate states (the people, and especially those responsible for the government of states), just as positive civil laws, enacted for the common good of the state, bind in conscience the citizens of the state.

> These moral obligations can, finally, furnish the basis of juridic obligations or positive law: they enable a juridic order to be constituted within international society. . . .
>
> When the exigencies of the common good are expressed in positive rules, these become law that binds the States, as the law binds the conscience of the individual citizen in any particular state.[80]

D.   SANCTIONS, OR COERCIVE POWER.

If the very notion of public authority implies the power to judge and to legislate, it also by its very nature must possess the power to enforce its decisions and laws. The latter is contained in the former as the necessary means to achieve the end, for a decision or law which has no binding

---

[79] *Summa Theol.*, I, II, q. 95, a. 2.

[80] Delos, "Christian Principles and International Relations," in *International Relations from a Catholic Standpoint*, pp. 50-51.

force or sanction is no more than a recommendation, an admonition to be accepted or rejected at will. Hence, St. Thomas says that law by its very nature implies two things: first, that it is a rule of human actions, and secondly that it has coercive power.[81]

Applied to the organized society of states, the necessity of coercive power immediately raises the question of international sanctions. It is at once evident that if the organized society of states is to have authority to render decisions on international questions and to legislate for the common good of all states, it must also possess the power to enforce these decisions and enactments by means of effective sanctions. The nature of these sanctions will vary according to the conception of international society that one has. Comparing the organic society of states of Vitoria with the inorganic world community of Suarez, Scott writes:

> In both a sanction is contemplated. In the one, it is a legal and a physical sanction, the authority of the world supported by law and expressed through physical means. In the other, the sanction is a moral and spiritual force, which, also supported by law, is based fundamentally, however, not on physical action but upon the moral principle which underlies all human relationship, good faith.[82]

It is with the organic, rationally organized society of states of Vitoria—the Thomistic concept of international society—that we are here concerned as the type of world community which is at once both objective and realistic. Hence, it is important that the principles underlying this conception of international society be carried to their logical conclusion, even if such conclusion run counter to the views entertained in many circles. One such conclusion is the necessity of physical as well as legal sanctions as the ex-

---

[81] Lex de sui ratione duo habet: primo quidem quod est regula humanorum actuum; secundo quod habet vim coactivam.—*Summa Theol.*, I, II, q. 96, a. 5.

[82] Scott, J. B., *The Catholic Conception of International Law*, p. 484.

pression of the coercive power within the organized society of states.   Physical sanctions in the last resort mean military sanctions.   Although economic and similar sanctions should be considered the more normal expression of international coercive power, yet military sanctions, even though the mere mention of them be offensive to idealists, must be reckoned with in any realistic conception of an organized society of states.   On this crucial point, Father Muller writes :

> While not overlooking the many difficulties to be faced in this solution, we hold that it is not possible to envisage a rational or effective organization of a League of Nations without giving a proper place to sanctions. No authority of any kind will be respected if it has no means of enforcing obedience. He who refuses to submit to the force of law must submit to the compulsion of force.
>
> It is true that it has been objected that there would be a contradiction if violence were placed at the disposal of law, if resort were had to war to bring about the reign of peace and if it were desired to establish order under cover of that disorder which is always let loose when resort is had to arms.   This objection is not apposite.   There is no question of basing the order of law on a reign of force, but of defending law against the attacks of unjust violence.   Far from overturning the order of peace, force, placed at the disposal of law unjustly attacked, brings an end to disorder and restores peace broken by the malice of the unjust aggressor.   This was the sense in which Benedict XV understood sanctions and in his message of peace of August 1st, 1917 (i.e., Letter to the leaders of the belligerent peoples) provided for sanctions to be taken against any State which either refused to submit international questions to arbitration, as an indispensable corollary to a general convention of arbitration and conciliation.[83]

This conclusion as to the necessity of physical coercive power in any effectively organized society of states is borne

[83] Muller, A., "The Organization of International Society," in *The Foundations of International Order*, p. 67.

out by the events of the past two decades. Nicholas Murray Butler again states the case very bluntly:

> The lesson taught by the League of Nations since its history began is that it was without the power to provide an effective police force to preserve order in the world out upon which it looked. Even the most law-abiding of peoples require a trained and ready police to meet those emergencies which no one can foresee and which, if not met, become invitations to new disorder and new crime.[84]

It is only in the light of recent events that the statement of William Rappard, previously quoted, can be properly evaluated, namely, that an international society built upon a purely subjective, voluntaristic judicial basis, lacking real legislative and coercive power, is helpless to maintain peace and order in the world of conflicting interests.[85] It is only in the light of modern world events also that the real significance of Vitoria's objective and organic conception of the world community of states can be fully appreciated. In the conclusion of his scholarly work on Francis of Vitoria, which has been included by the Carnegie Endowment for International Peace among its "Classics of International Law," Dr. James Brown Scott gives us an admirable appreciation of Vitoria and his doctrine in the light of modern international institutions and recent world trends. The significance of Dr. Scott's words will more than justify the length of the quotation.

> The corner-stone of Victoria's system was equality of States, applicable not merely to the States of Christendom and of Europe but also to the barbarian principalities in the Western World of Columbus. The modern State is looked upon from within and from without. From within it is a thing of constitutional law; from without, of international law. From within it must be self-

[84] Butler, Nicholas Murray, *Toward a Federal World,* An address delivered at the Parrish Art Museum, Southampton, Long Island, September 3, 1939, p. 12.

[85] Rappard, Wm. E., "Du Fédéralisme international," *L'Esprit International,* no. 54, Jan. 1940, p. 11.

sufficient, in order to be a perfect State; from
without it is but a member of the international
community.   These are precisely the elements to
be found in Victoria's conception of the State. ...

'Many men, many minds' is a proverbial way of
saying that people united in society differ individually.   The differences result in disputes between members of the groups and controveries be-
the groups which are called States.   Within the
State these disputes are not redressed by the individual themselves, although they may protect
their lives or their property against immediate attack, but are laid before a court in which justice
is done, property restored or damages awarded—
or both—and punishment administered whenever
the act is of a criminal nature.   Here again the
fundamental Victorian doctrine and the modern
practice are at once.

But the groups, made up as they are of people,
may differ and their controversies must needs be
adjusted. These controversies should be settled in
the same way as the disputes between individuals,
because they are not disputes of the artificial
things called States, but of the peoples forming
them.   Therefore the same principles of justice apply to both.   It follows that force between States
could only justly be used to redress a wrong, and a
resort to force was only to be tolerated because
there was no court of the States;   for the States
being equal, there could be no court of the superior
in the same way that there were tribunals within
each State.   This is the Victorian conception.   Un-
happily it has not been embodied in the practice of
the centuries that followed him.

The creation of an international court of justice
by the States and for the States, in which their
controversies could be decided in the same manner
as within the State, would render war both un-
necessary and unlawful.   The Permanent Court of
International Justice, established but a decade ago,
upon the initiative of the successors of Victoria's
aborigines, is the culmination of that phase of his
system of international law.

But there are the States and a larger State, an international community, existing by the mere co-existence of the States, even though there be no formal organization. Before Columbus discovered the American Indies, the States of Christendom—the European world—were the international community. It was Victoria's judgement, ever a liberal one, that the American principalities—as equals of the Christian States—should not be excluded from this international community. Therefore in his theory of international law, they were members possessing the same rights and the same duties as the Christian States of Europe. In Victoria's conception, the international community, composed of States without reference to geography, race, or religion, replaced the large but still limited international community coextensive with Christendom; this is the opinion of the world today.

But this is but a part of Victoria's law of nations. The international community is not a super-imposed State; it is coextensive with humanity—no longer merely with Christianity. It is composed of the States and is their representative; it is likewise the representative of the common humanity rather than of the common religion binding the States. It is a union of the States, and the sum total of the States is necessarily more powerful than any of its parts. Its will is the will of humanity, speaking in terms of peoples; its will is international law, speaking in terms of States. But this law reaches the individual through the State, and it controls the actions of the States in their relations with one another.

The international community, therefore, in the Victorian system, possesses the inherent right to impose its will—in the form of law applicable to the individual State—and to punish its violation, not because of a treaty, of a pact or a covenant, but because of an international need. For just as the State is not a 'perfect' State if it be not self-sufficient, so would the international community be imperfect if could not impose its collective judgement, in the form of the law of nations, upon humanity—considered as such—and upon the States

as members of the international community. All
this is not merely a consequence of Victoria's doctrine; it is the doctrine itself expressly and un-
mistakably stated in classical terms four centuries
before our modern world endeavored to create by
covenant what Victoria had proclaimed as a fundamental principle and which we would call the culmination of his law of nations.[86]

[86] Scott, James Brown, *The Spanish Origin of International Law,
Part I: Francisco de Vitoria and his Law of Nations*, pp. 281-283.
(Reprinted by permission of the Carnegie Endowment for Inter-
national Peace.)

CHAPTER IV

INDIVIDUAL STATES AND THE SOCIETY OF STATES.

I. THE RELATION OF THE INDIVIDUAL STATE TO THE SOCIETY AS A WHOLE.

In every organized society there exists a set of reciprocal relations, of parts to the whole, and vice-versa, of the whole to the parts—the relation of the individual members to the society as a whole, and the relation of the society to its individual members. In Thomistic philosophy of society these relations are not oppositional, but unitary, for these relations of members to the whole and vice-versa are not conceived as a "conflict" between the individual and the community, but rather as an integration of the two, as the proper "ordering" of the individual members to the whole community, and on the other hand, of the community as a whole to the individual members.

As in every other organized society, so also in the society of states there exists this set of reciprocal relations—of the individual states to the community of states, and the whole society of states to the individual member states. The individual member states have certain functions to perform towards the whole community of states, and likewise this total community has its proper functions towards the individual member states. In the preceding chapter we have noted how, in the Thomistic concept of society, these relations flow out of the recognition of a universal common good, as a consequence of which individual states have certain moral obligations and functions to realize this common good, including the organization of a specific society for the achievement of this purpose, and granted this organization, the positive society of states which is thus brought into being also acquires certain specific functions towards the states singly and collectively, for the proper performance of which adequate power and authority are requisite, in

133

order that thus the universal common good may be effectively secured.   Underlying this whole concept of reciprocal
relations and functions is the Thomistic notion of order
and the principle of "ordering" (to be understood, of course,
in the sense of bringing about order) of the members to
the common good of the whole.[1]

In recent centuries, unfortunately, the idea of "conflict"
has all too frequently supplanted the Thomistic notion of
"order" in societal relations.   Examples of conflict between
the individual and the state in modern absolutist political
theory and practice are numerous enough, but with these
we are not concerned here.   It is rather with the consequence of these theories and their application to the relation
of individual states to the collectivity of states that we are
concerned.   There is a manifest conflict between the concept
of an organic society of states and certain modern notions
of the state which attribute to the state prerogatives which
it does not rightfully possess, such as complete independence
of the state from any authority outside of the state, unlimited powers in external as well as internal matters, ultimate perfection in the social and political order.   Although
this false notion of the state is the product of many factors,
philosophical, political, social, economic, cultural, and racial,
all of which can be conveniently summed up in the one term
"excessive nationalism," there are two underlying concepts
which stand out in the historical development of this notion
and bear investigation: the concept of the state as a
"perfect society," and the concept of sovereignty.   Around
these two points, both of which are closely related, revolves
the whole problem of the relation of the individual states
to the society of states.   These two points will therefore
be considered in their modern significance and correlated
with the Thomistic notions, for between the Thomistic concept of the state and the concept of the society of states
there is no conflict, but rather a relation of integration, both
together forming one integral political order.   After con-

[1] *Summa Theol.*, I, q. 108, a. 4; I, II, q. 90, a. 3; II, II, q. 58, a. 5.

sidering the relation of the individual state to the whole society of states under the two points just mentioned, namely, the notion of the state as a "perfect society" and the concept of state sovereignty, we shall conclude the chapter by a brief consideration of the whole society in relation to the individual states.

A.   THE NOTION OF THE STATE AS A "PERFECT SOCIETY."

"To consider the State as something ultimate to which everything else should be subordinated and directed, cannot fail to harm the true and lasting prosperity of nations."[2] Thus Pope Pius XII characterizes a prevalent fallacious notion of the state as "perfect society"—perfect in the sense of being the ultimate in the social and political order, the source of all authority and the end to which all things are subordinated.   Being perfect in this sense means that the state is complete master of all its affairs, whether internal or external, taking directions from no outside authority, submitting to no compromise of its freedom of action, save by voluntary pact revocable at will.   It means that even if the state cannot remain economically isolated and independent of other states, especially under modern world conditions, it is nevertheless completely isolated and independent politically.   The individual state has the last word in anything that pertains to its affairs.   This evidently is extreme individualism in international affairs, a survival of that extreme individualism which dominated social, economic, and political matters within the state for nearly two centuries.   It is evident, too, that such an extremely individualistic notion of the state as a completely self-contained, independent "perfect society" is altogether incompatible with the concept of an organic society of states.   Hence, to say the least, "the tendency to attribute to the national state alone the character of a perfect society full panoplied with authority needs to undergo some modifications."[3]

[2] Pope Pius XII, Encyclical Letter *Summi Pontificatus*.
[3] *The World Society*, p. 10.

St. Thomas also designated the state as a "perfect society," but his use of the term was quite different from that described in the preceding paragraph. But the term is no longer applicable to the state in exactly the same manner in which St. Thomas used it, for, in the centuries that have lapsed since his time, the state has been greatly modified, particularly in its relations with other states, as the result of world-wide economic, cultural, and political changes. A corresponding modification has taken place in the notion of the state as a perfect society. Delos thus describes it:

> Formerly it was the tendency of jurists and of the law to lay stress especially on the independence of states. Inspired by the teaching of Aristotle, legal doctrine saw in the state—the city—a self-sufficing community. St. Thomas defines it: a society which procures for its members the complete good of human life. Such a society should normally suffice for all human needs, and seems, therefore, to be essentially independent. This conception corresponded adequately enough to the facts of the case, as long as the state of civilization lasted in which most countries could live almost entirely each on its own resources, only luxuries and articles of secondary importance being imported from abroad. And so, in determining the rights and duties of states, jurists and moralists reasoned from the data: the state is a self-sufficing community. But we must be careful before deducing from this the right of absolute independence or isolation.

> In this conception there is room only for inter-individual moral relations between states. But the absolute independence of political societies, never perfectly realized, is today more than ever a dream. The very first of Catholic thinkers who saw before them the modern national state, recognized that it could not be self-sufficing.[4]

[4] Delos, "Christian Principles and International Relations," in *International Relations from a Catholic Standpoint*, pp. 43-44.

If we examine the political philosophy of Aristotle, we shall note that he indeed regarded the state as a self-sufficing community; it was this in fact which distinguished the state from lower social groups. "When several villages are united in a single complete community, large enough to be nearly or quite self-sufficing, the state comes into existence, originating in the bare needs of life, and continuing in existence for the sake of a good life."[5] Aristotle consequently describes the state as "a community of families and aggregations of families in well-being, for the sake of a perfect and self-sufficing life," or again as "the union of families and villages in a perfect and self-sufficing life, by which we mean a happy and honourable life."[6]

But from the context of these passages, it is evident that Aristotle is not speaking of the state as a "perfect society" in the sense of a completely autonomous and independent political unit, but rather of the state as a "self-sufficing" community from the economic, social, or cultural point of view. It should be noted that a fundamental principle of Aristotle's political philosophy is that "a state exists for the sake of a good life, and not for the sake of life only."[7] For Aristotle this "good life" means, not merely material welfare, but especially that higher well-being or happiness which comes from the practice of the intellectual and moral virtues, for the exercise of which material welfare is only the necessary means. A society is regarded as perfect or self-sufficing only if it is capable of providing for this "good life." The family and the village in the opinion of Aristotle cannot do this, whereas the state can; it is for this reason that the state is regarded as a perfect and self-sufficing community. This is not to deny that this community should be self-governing. Although Aristotle does not expressly mention this condition, namely that a self-sufficing community should be self-governing, this is implied in his whole system of political philosophy and in the very notion of a "good

[5] Aristotle, *Politics*, I, 2, 1252b 27-30.
[6] *Ibid.*, III, 9, 1280b 33, 1281a 1.
[7] *Ibid.*, III, 9, 1280a 31.

life." Yet, in his characterization of the state as a "self-sufficing" community, Aristotle does not ascribe to it the prerogatives which have frequently been claimed by the modern national state, and it seems safe to say that a state which makes adequate provision for the economic, social, cultural, and moral welfare of its citizens, even though it is not absolutely autonomous and independent politically, corresponds more closely to Aristotle's notion of a "self-sufficing community" than would a state which is absolutely independent politically but incapable of providing adequately for the well-being of its own citizens.

In his commentary on the *Politics* of Aristotle, St. Thomas repeatedly designates the state as a "perfect community," even as the "most perfect" of human societies. But it is apparent at once that his meaning is similar to that of Aristotle, with perhaps even less emphasis on the completeness of the self-sufficiency. Thus he says, that while every human society is ordained to provide for some necessity of life, that is a perfect community which is capable of making sufficient provision for all the *necessities of life.*[8]

There is a significant passage in *De Regimine Principum,* which, although already quoted and discussed at some length in Chapter II, bears repetition here for the light that it throws on St. Thomas' designation of the state as a perfect community, and on the approach which he took to this problem.

[8] Civitas est communitas perfecta ... quia cum omnis communicatio omnium hominum ordinetur ad aliquid necessarium vitae, illa erit perfecta communitas quae ordinatur ad hoc quod homo habeat sufficienter quicquid est necessarium ad vitam: talis autem communitas est civitas. Est enim de ratione civitatis quod in ea inveniantur omnia quae sufficiunt ad vitam humanam, sicut contingit esse—*In Polit.*, I, 1.

Civitas nihil est aliud quam multitudo talium, qui sic dicuntur cives, ut per se sufficienter vivere possint simpliciter. Est enim civitas communitas per se sufficiens.—*Ibid.*, III, 1.

Quarum quidem communitatum cum diversi sint gradus et ordines, ultima est communitas civitatis ordinata ad per se sufficientia vitae humanae. Unde inter omnes communitates humanas ipsa est perfectissima.—*Ibid.*, I, 1.

Now, since men must live in a group, because they are not sufficient unto themselves to procure the necessities of life were they to remain solitary, it follows that a society will be the more perfect the more it is sufficient unto itself to procure the necessities of life. There is, indeed; to some extent sufficiency for life in one family of one household, namely in so far as pertains to the natural acts of nourishment and the begetting of offspring and other things of this kind; it exists, furthermore, in one village with regard to those things which belong to one trade; but it exists in a city, which is a perfect community, with regard to all the necessities of life; but still more in a province because of the need of fighting together and of mutual help against enemies.[9]

It is clear from the words of St. Thomas, as well as from the context, that the state is here considered as a "perfect community" primarily from the economic point of view. Considering the economic conditions of his time, the thirteenth century, St. Thomas finds that the city-state (*civitas*, the city with its surrounding country side) is capable of providing sufficiently for the material welfare of its citizens, and is therefore entitled to the designation of a "perfect community." It is only when he comes to the province that political and military notions are introduced: although the province may not make any better economic provision than the city (considering the times), yet it does contribute to the "good life" indirectly by providing greater security and protection, and thus is a "still more perfect community."

St. Thomas summarizes his views on the matter very

[9] Cum autem homini competat in multitudine vivere, quia sibi non sufficit ad necessaria vitae, si solitarius maneat, oportet quod tanto sit perfectior multitudinis societas, quanto magis per se sufficiens erit ad necessaria vitae. Habetur siquidem aliqua vitae sufficientia, in una familia domus unius, quantum scilicet ad naturales actus nutritionis, et prolis generandae, et aliorum hujusmodi; in uno autem vico, quantum ad ea quae ad unum artificium pertinent; in civitate vero, quae est perfecta communitas, quantum ad omnia necessaria vitae; sed adhuc magis in provincia una propter necessitatem compugnationis et mutui auxilii contra hostes.—*De Reg. Prin.*, Lib. I, cap. 1.

succinctly in his *Commentary on the Gospel of St. Matthew.* Here he distinguishes three types of communities: the family, the city, and the kingdom. The city (*civitas*) is a "perfect community" only in the sense that it provides for the "mere necessities of life" (*quantum ad mere necessaria*). But the kingdom (or province) inasmuch as it provides greater security is the *"communitas consummationis."*[10]

From the foregoing it is quite apparent that when St. Thomas spoke of the state as a "perfect community" he had in mind primarily its economic self-sufficiency as the necessary means for the development of the higher "good life." Again, as in the case of Aristotle, this is not to deny that St. Thomas regarded the political power of the state to govern its citizens as a necessary requisite for a "perfect community." In fact, he expressly uses the term in connection with the public political power of the state to legislate and to govern the families and citizens under its jurisdiction.[11] But certainly from the political point of view St. Thomas never conceived the state as a "perfect society" in the sense of being supreme and ultimate in the hierarchy of human values, as absolutely autonomous and independent in its internal and external affairs. Such a concept is completely at variance with the whole political philosophy of St. Thomas, as will be pointed out when discussing the notion of sovereignty.

From the economic viewpoint, Aristotle's and St. Thomas' notions of the state as a self-sufficing or perfect community did accord well enough with the facts of the case, considering the economic conditions of the times, in which

[10] Triplex est communitas: domus sive familiae, civitatis, et regni. Domus est consistens ex his per quos fiunt communes actus: ideo consistit ex triplici conjugatione: ex patre et filio; ex marito et uxore; ex domino et servo. Communitas civitatis omnia continet quae ad vitam hominis necessaria: unde est perfecta communitas quantum ad mere necessaria. Tertia communitas est regni, quae est communitas consummationis.—*Expositio in Evangelium S. Matthaei*, cap. 12.

[11] *Summa Theol.*, I, II, q. 90, a. 3, ad 3.

people depended almost exclusively upon their own resources for their livelihood. But these notions do not apply today as they did at that time for the simple reason that the facts themselves have undergone a radical change. Indeed the movement towards economic interdependence between peoples began in the later mediaeval period, in which St. Thomas lived, chiefly as the result of the Crusades and the contact of Europe with the East, and received a great impetus in the fifteenth and sixteenth centuries owing to the rapid succession of world-wide discoveries during that era. Thus the closed economy of the city and province gave way to an open economy, a flow of commerce between cities, provinces, and the new national states which were then in the process of formation. Those who witnessed these changes realized that even these national states could not be economically independent and self-sufficing in the sense of the old city-states. An indication of this can be detected in a passage from Suarez.

> Therefore, although a given sovereign state, commonwealth, or kingdom, may constitute a perfect community in itself, consisting of its own members, nevertheless, each one of these states is also, in a certain sense, and viewed in relation to the human race, a member of that universal society; for these states when standing alone are never so self-sufficient that they do not require some mutual assistance, association, and intercourse, at times for their own greater welfare and advantage, but at other times because also of some moral necessity or need. This fact is made manifest by actual usage.[12]

In the interim, consequently, the very notion of the state as a "perfect community" had undergone a change. A difference in approach is apparent. This is evident in the passage just quoted from Suarez. It is also noticeable in

---

[12] Suarez, Francisco, *De Legibus ac Deo Legislatore*, Lib. II, cap. 19, no. 9. (English translation reprinted from Scott, *Law, the State, and the International Community*, II, p. 257, by permission of Columbia University Press.)

the writings of Vitoria : he too regards the state as a "perfect society" in its political and juridical aspect, not in the sense of an economically "self-sufficing" community. A state is a perfect community if it is a complete political unit, possessing the power of internal self-government, and is therefore not a part of some other state and dependant upon it. A community which lacks these essential qualifications lacks something essential, and is therefore imperfect.

> Now the whole difficulty is in the questions: What is a State, and who can properly be called a sovereign prince? I will briefly reply to them by saying that a State is properly called a perfect community. But the essence of the difficulty is in saying what a perfect community is. By way of solution be it noted that a thing is called perfect when it is a completed whole, for that is imperfect in which there is something wanting and, on the other hand, that is perfect from which nothing is wanting. A perfect State or community, therefore, is one which is complete in itself, that is, which is not a part of another community, but has its own laws and its own council and its own magistrates, such as is the Kingdom of Castile and Aragon and the Republic of Venice and other of the like. For there is no obstacle to many principalities and perfect States being under one prince.[13]

"In other words, the test of whether a given political community is a state or not is its indepedence of other political communities, its indepedent self-government, its *juridical* self-sufficiency."[14]

This "juridical self-sufficiency," or independent self-government, in the philosophy of Vitoria, does not mean that the state has absolute autonomy and independence. In the mind of Vitoria, it is necessary to distinguish two aspects

---

[13] Vitoria, Francisco de, *De Jure Belli*, 425-426.

[14] Wright, Herbert, "Vitoria and the State," in *Francisco de Vitoria: Addresses in Commemoration of the Fourth Centenary of his lectures "De Indis" and "De Jure Belli,"* delivered at the Catholic University of America, May 1, 1932, Washington, 1932, p. 26.

of the state: its internal organization and its external relations. Considered in its internal organization, a state to be perfect must have authority over its members and a complete machinery of government; hence it is not part of some larger political unit through which its internal affairs are administered. On the other hand, considered in its external relations, it is not necessary for a state to be indepedent of any outside authority in order to be a perfect community. In fact Vitoria states expressly that there is no obstacle to many perfect states being under one ruler. Indeed elsewhere he concedes that the states of Christendom have the right to elect a common ruler, and even that the states of the world have the right to designate a single world authority.[15]By making this concession Vitoria is not thereby depriving the individual states of their prerogative of being perfect communities in the sense in which he understood the term. Dr. Scott thus sums up Vitoria's position:

> From the internal point of view, therefore, Vitoria's state is a "perfect community." Externally, however, it is but one state among many, not sufficient unto itself, but a member, upon an equal footing with other states, of the international community.[16]

Thus it is obvious that the notion of the state as a "perfect society" has undergone a transformation, at least in emphasis and approach, during the course of Thomistic tradition. This, however, does not imply any change in the fundamental principles regarding the Thomistic philosophy of the state. The false designation of the state as a "perfect society" in the sense of its being absolutely autonomous and independent is equally at variance with the principles of St. Thomas and those of Vitoria and of all Thomistic political philosophy. Granted, however, the permanence of these fundamental principles, it seems necessary to modify

---

[15] *De Potestate Civili*, 204, 206.

[16] Scott, James Brown, "Vitoria and International Law," in *Francisco de Vitoria*, Addresses delivered at the Catholic University of America, p. 39.

more and more the notion of the state as a "perfect community" in proprotion to the growing interdependence of states resulting from modern economic, cultural, and political circumstances. This is the view taken by the contributors to *A Code of International Ethics.*

> For a long time the fact that nations were widely scattered and consequently lived in isolation, has prevented any considerable and fruitful international collaboration from taking place, and philosophers and moralists alike came to consider the State as a *perfect society,* endowed with all the necessary means to help its members to attain "the full good of human life."
>
> Things are very different to-day. In view of the great extension of international life the term *perfect society* can only be applied to the State in a very restricted sense.
>
> The State is still a perfect society, inasmuch as it possesses full authority to maintain order, peace and justice within its boundaries, since a universal State which could claim immediate jurisdiction over all members of the human family is almost unthinkable.
>
> But the State is no longer a perfect society inasmuch as it cannot now give to its subjects, by its own means, the "fullest good of human life," such as the progress of civilization and the fruitful resources of an harmoniously organized international co-operation have rendered possible.[17]

So far as the false modern notion of the state as a "perfect society" (as opposed to the Thomistic notion) is concerned, certainly a change in attitude is necessary if states are to cooperate harmoniously with one another. Hence, we may conclude:

> The tendency to attribute to the national state alone the character of a perfect society full panoplied with authority needs to undergo some modifications. The perfection attainable and required for the modern state is not to be found solely in national communities but most eminently in world society and a Commonwealth of Nations.

[17] *A Code of International Ethics,* p. 14.

At least some of the attributes of sovereignty and authority must be transferred to a world organization if the world of today is to solve its problems in the most efficacious fashion and if the moral ends of the political community are to be better approximated.[18]

This leads us to our next point: the concept of state sovereignty.

B.   SOVEREIGNTY.

Intimately connected with the notion of the state as a perfect society is the concept of the sovereignty or political power of the state. This concept of sovereignty has likewise undergone a radical transformation during the course of centuries. Although some measure of sovereignty or public authority is essential to the proper functioning of states, yet the notion of state sovereignty in its modern exaggerated form constitutes perhaps the greatest single obstacle to the peaceful and harmonious cooperation of states and their organization into an effective society of states. This is the conclusion expressed by Nicholas Murray Butler, after a brief survey of the rôle of state sovereignty in recent world events.

What is the lesson to be learned from all this? Surely it is now the clear demonstration of more than a thousand years of nation-building that the doctrine of national sovereignty is both unsound and dangerous. That doctrine can only lead, as it has led, to the notion that each and every established government is a law unto itself and not subject to any limitations or control in its dealings with other governments. Put bluntly, this means that when two of these so-called sovereign governments cannot agree upon any matter which affects them both, then recourse shall be had to force, which is war. Constituted as they are, human beings in control of the administration of governments that claim to be sovereign will be constantly at war, regardless of the loss of life or of property

[18] *The World Society*, p. 10.

which must always accompany war, whether successful or unsuccessful.[19]

As a qualification of the statement just quoted, it must be noted that not every doctrine of state sovereignty is "unsound and dangerous"; but certainly that doctrine which Dr. Butler describes—"the notion that each and every established government is a law unto itself and not subject to any limitations"—which is characteristic of the modern concept of national state sovereignty, is "both unsound and dangerous." There is a sound doctrine of the public power or authority of the state (sovereignty in the acceptable sense of the term) which is based objectively on the nature of man and the end of the state—the common good, the very notion of which involves far-reaching limitations on the exercise of public power and authority of the state. This is the Thomistic concept of sovereignty. But the modern notion of sovereignty, instead of being solidly objective, is rather subjective and legalistic, based on an expression of will or consent and in keeping with the modern concept of law; limitations, if any, are consequently also subjective, not arising from an objective moral, social, and political order. To realize the difference between these two doctrines it will be advantageous to trace briefly the development of the modern notion of sovereignty and then contrast it with the Thomistic concept of public power and authority in the state.

By way of introduction, the position of Aristotle in this matter should be noted. According to him, the state, as we have seen should be self-sufficient, which implied that as a condition for its realization of the "good life" the state should possess its own government and a supreme command. But this supreme command, as Professor McIlwain points out, is not the same as sovereignty in the modern sense.

> It is natural to identify this supreme power (τὸ κύριον) with our modern sovereignty... and the class enjoying it with our "sovereign"; but this is

[19] Butler, Nicholas Murray, *Toward a Federal World*, pp. 3-4.

very questionable. For modern sovereignty is a legalistic conception, the outgrowth of the ideas of Roman law, and their application to modern national states; Aristotle's discussion of "supremacy" here is nothing but an "ethico-political appraisal" of the relation of the "political koinonia" to other lesser associations of men. It is no manifestation of the supreme authority in the state defined in terms of law that he is thinking, but of an actual supremacy in an economic and social class ensured by physical authority.[20]

In this passage Professor McIlwain gives the clue to the modern notion of sovereignty as a "legalistic conception" which is "the outgrowth of the ideas of the Roman law and their application to modern national states." According to the conception of the old Roman law, the power to rule was considered as being held originally by the Roman people and transferred by them voluntarily, though completely and irrevocably, to the rulers through the *lex regia.* It was especially under the Empire that this concept was elaborated to justify the tenure of sovereign power by the emperor. "The Roman emperors had been obsessed with the conception of *imperium,* that is, the power to govern conferred by the *lex regia,* which, in the view of the Roman jurists, transferred to the emperor the power which the people had possessed in their republican institutions."[21]

But in the Middle Ages a new political order came into being, in which the law was above the king, especially the universal law of Christianity which formed the bond of a united Christendom, and consequently the notion of sovereignty in the Roman sense was temporarily lost sight of. Towards the end of the mediaeval period, however, political conditions began to change and the old questions of "government by supremacy or government by law" were raised

[20] McIlwain, Charles Howard, *The Growth of Political Thought in the West,* pp. 80-81. (Reprinted by permission of the Macmillan Company, publishers.)

[21] Scott, James Brown, *Law, the State, and the International Community,* I, p. 332.

again.[22]   It was under these circumstances that the political theory of the old Roman law and its concept of sovereignty were revived.

Yet throughout the mediaeval period the Roman idea of imperium had survived in the universal *Respublica Christiana*, in which, at least in theory, temporal power over all Christendom was held by the emperor—a theory which was given the official sanction of the Church through the coronation of Charlemagne by Pope Leo III.   But this temporal power was circumscribed by the numerous restrictions imposed by law in all its mediaeval comprehensiveness.   The emperor indeed was nominally the sovereign ruler of the *Respublica Christiana*, but his sovereignty must be appraised in the light of mediaeval political theory and practice.   Even in the most influential days of the Carolingian and Holy Roman Empire, whole peoples remained outside the orbit of the emperor's authority;   yet among all Christians, the emperor held at least the rank and dignity of being the supreme temporal ruler of Christendom. But when mediaeval universalism was breaking up and powerful new nation-states began to appear, the notion of sovereignty was transferred, under the influence of the political theories revived from the old Roman law, from the emperor to the individual kings of these states.   Each king or ruler came to be considered the sovereign in his own realm, just as the emperor was (or had been) in the entire *Respublica Christiana*.   Already in the fourteenth century this changed concept of sovereignty is evident in the legalistic formulas current at the time: "The king has as much power over his people as the Emperor has over the whole of Christendom;" "The king of France is the emperor in his own realm."[23] Thus it was by a simple transposition of the title of sovereign with its prerogatives from one universal ruler to the

[22] *Ibid.*, I, p. 343.
[23] "Tantam potestatem habet in populo quantum Imperator in universo."   "Le roi de France est empereur en son royaume."—quoted from Delos, *La société internationale et les principles du droit public,* p. 191.

kings of the new national states that the modern concept of national sovereignty came into being.[24]

With the secession of the new national states from the universal Empire, and the transposition of the title and prerogatives of sovereign from the emperor to the rulers of these states, went hand in hand the development of the spirit of independence and isolation and the tendency of the state to centralize and absorb everything into itself. Thus Laski describes this process:

> The state becomes self-sufficing, therefore to the state the unique allegiance of the individual is due. It ceases to think of superiority as existent outside itself. The state is that which has no superior, wherefore all other forms of social organization, as guilds for example, are subject to its control. The dawning sense of nationalism was at hand to give that concept an enviable sharpness of definition. There was thenceforth to be no lord of the world, imperial or otherwise, for the simple reason that there was no single world. There was England, France, and Spain. The life of each was to be centralized within its ultimate sovereign.[25]

Permeating this process was the theory of rule and sovereignty, subjective and voluntaristic, derived from the old Roman law. Although the legists continued to hold in theory the popular origin of sovereignty, yet since its trans-

[24] Le jour où sur les ruines de l'Empire se constituèrent des États nouveaux où des nations plus homogènes et cohérentes sortirent de la poussière du monde féodal, il fullut détacher l'idée de souveraineté de la personne de l'Empereur, longtemps son unique titulaire, pour la reporter avec ses prérogatives sur la tête de rois nouveaux. Les Légistes s'y employèrent deux siècles durant, mais la transposition semble achevée au début du XIVe siècle.

C'est en effet par une simple transposition que le problème de la souveraineté nationale est résolu. La souveraineté imperiale devient souveraineté royale sans transformation profonde ni réelle de l'idée de souveraineté. On se borne, pourrait-on dire, à la reporter d'une tête sur une autre, de l'empereur au souverain nouveau.—*Ibid.*, pp. 190-191.

[25] Laski, Harold J., *The Foundations of Sovereignty*, New York: Harcourt, Brace and Company, 1921, p. 13.

mission to the king was complete and irrevocable, rule became tantamout to the expression of the ruler's will: *jus est quod jussum est.*[26] Since the ruler was a source of law, he was above the law.   It was the opinion of two of the greatest legists of the fourteenth century that while the ruler "ought" to comply with the law, in reality he was above the law—*legibus solutus.*[27]

So long as this principle was applied solely to the positive law of the state, the effects might not have been so disastrous, but when the ruler was regarded as freed from the restrictions of the natural law in his public acts, as he was by Machiavelli, and from certain precepts of the divine positive law, as he was by Luther and other "reformers," the result could only be an absolute supremacy over both subjects and law—an absolute sovereignty.[28]   In fact, it was during the religious and political turmoil of the sixteenth century that the theory of sovereignty in its modern form was expounded by Jean Bodin, who defined sovereignty as "supreme power over citizens and subjects, unrestrained by laws."[29]   Although Bodin still held in theory the obligation of the ruler's submission to natural and divine positive law, yet these limitations were greatly over-shadowed by his insistence on the greatest prerogative and highest privilege of sovereignty which "consists primarily in giving laws not only to individuals but also to the people as a whole without their consent."[30]   No bolder statement of absolute soverignty could be made than that set down by a contemporary of Bodin, Alberico Gentili:

> This, then, is the characteristic of sovereignty, that the principate shall never at any time recognize anything as superior to itself, neither man nor law.   Therefore this power is both absolute and

[26] *Ibid.,* p. 17.

[27] Scott, *Law, The State, and the International Community,* I, p. 343.

[28] *Ibid.,* I, p. 344; Laski, *op. cit.,* pp. 15-16.

[29] "Maiestas est summa in cives ac subditos legibusque soluta potestas."—quoted from Scott, *Law, the State, and the International Community,* I, p. 332.

[30] *Ibid.,* I, p. 338.

without limit. "The prince is *legibus solutus*" will be the law, and whatever is pleasing to the prince will be the same as law.[31]

From such a concept of sovereignty to the absolutism of a Louis XIV of France or a James I of England is but a simple and logical step.

So far we have considered the concept of sovereignty primarily from within: the supreme power of the ruler in his own realm and over his own subjects—internal sovereignty. But it was only natural and logical to apply this concept of sovereignty also to the external relations of the state with other states—external sovereignty. The definition of sovereignty by Gentili, who also enjoys the reputation of being one of the pioneers of international law, indicates the significance of this concept in interstate relations, since "the principate shall never at any time recognize anything as superior to itself, neither man nor law." Even Grotius himself, who has long been regarded as the father of international law, held a concept of sovereignty which was in the end to prove disastrous to that very peace and order in the world which he strove so hard to establish. This is not a personal opinion, but the view of an eminent English jurist. His words are truly significant, even though his conclusions have been marred by another World War.

> And so a jurist may be forgiven for suggesting that, whatever may have been the case in the past, the theory of sovereignty seems, at the present day, to be one of the greatest stumbling-blocks in the path of international progress. Its appearance in the international world is due preeminently to two men, Bodin and Grotius. Bodin's motives may well be suspect. Those of Grotius were entirely honourable, and were at first crowned with brilliant success.... In order to make his thesis acceptable, he attempted to placate jealousies by releasing all

[31] Gentili, Alberico, *Regales disputationes tres, Disputatio prima.* (Translation reprinted from Scott, *Law, the State, and the International Community*, I, p. 345, by permission of Columbia University Press.)

States from any external human authority, that is, in accordance with the accepted views of the day, regarding them as being, so far as their intercourse with one another was concerned, in a "natural" or pre-political condition. And for that very reason, he urged, they were bound by the only law suitable for such a condition, viz. the Law of Nature, the "dictate of right reason."

Grotius' success was, at first, admittedly, brilliant. His *De Jure Belli ac Pacis* is, judged by its practical influence, one of the world's great books. . . . But the theory on which it was founded was, in fact, a toleration of anarchy; and, in due time, it collapsed, with the results which are painfully obvious. It is hardly too much to say that ever since the Great War, the world has been struggling to escape from the theory of sovereignty in international affairs—from its jealousies, its rivalries, its preposterous pretentions, and its apprehensions—and to build up out of the ruins left by the war, a more wholesome theory of international society.[32]

Undoubtedly the success which Grotius first achieved in international affairs was due to a great extent to the survival of the motion of natural law from earlier times as a moral law imposing ethical obligations and supported by moral sanctions. But, unfortunately, even this notion of natural law was repudiated, and anarchy in interstate relations became the normal condition of the world. In a passage on Hobbes' doctrine of sovereignty, in which law was regarded simply as the will and command of the sovereign, Cook indicates the effect of this subjective theory on international relations for succeeding centuries.

This is the very essence of the doctrine of sovereignty. It was to be developed by subsequent legal thinkers of the analytical school, particularly by Austin. It makes law such, simply in terms of its source, without regard to the function which law is to perform or to the justice or wisdom of par-

[32] Jenks, Edward, *The New Jurisprudence*, London: John Murray, 1933, pp. 82-84.

ticular laws. The whole idea that law is to be measured by ethical norms is rejected. Law is entirely divorced from ethics, as well as from the social setting in which it has to function. Yet this doctrine became the dominant theory of a subsequent period and a defense of the nation-state, both against its citizens and vis-à-vis other nations. It was largely responsible for the idea that man's prime duty as a citizen is unquestioning obedience to any law. Not only internally, but in the external international relations of states, it was to do infinite damage, for it denied the possibility of superior international authority and insisted that the sovereign state was beyond the reach of judgment. The latter alone could determine what were its interests in its dealings with other peoples.[33]

Such is the concept of state sovereignty that we of the twentieth century have inherited from the past. It is true that since the time of Bodin and Hobbes great changes have taken place in regard to state sovereignty, but these changes concern the location of sovereignty rather than the concept of sovereignty itself. The personal sovereignty of rulers, hedged about by numerous constitutional restrictions resulting from the democratic movements of the eighteenth and nineteenth centuries, has given way to the collective or impersonal sovereignty of the state. Yet the concept of the state as the highest authority, recognizing no superior either in its internal or external affairs, the source of law, and the final tribunal of judgment in all matters pertaining to it— the concept of unlimited state sovereignty—still remains. And even though this concept has been tempered to some extent in recent decades by the submission of international disputes in certain instances to an international tribunal and a closer cooperation between states before the present war, whether within or outside the League of Nations, the notion of unrestricted state sovereignty still prevails. The contemporary doctrine of state sovereignty in relation to

[33] Cook, Thomas I., *History of Political Philosophy from Plato to Burke*, New York: Prentice-Hall, 1936, pp. 503-504.

international affairs is thus described by Charles Fenwick
in his *International Law*.

> It is the absence of law governing the more
> fundamental interests of nations that explains the
> apparent contradiction between the sovereignty of
> states and the existence of rules of international
> law. The traditional theory of sovereignty implies
> the complete freedom of a state from control of
> any higher power claiming authority to regulate its
> acts. Whatever rules of conduct are recognized by
> the state as binding upon it must be self imposed
> obligations. . . . Sovereignty thus implies not the
> denial of rules of law already in existence, as has
> at times been its practical significance, but the re-
> jection of rules imposed by a higher authority
> against the will of the state. . . .
>
> When tested by the facts of international life it
> is seen that, on the one hand, sovereignty is com-
> patible with numerous restrictions upon state con-
> duct in matters in which the advantages of an
> orderly adjustment of claims, by adoption of a
> common rule of law, have come to be recognized.
> Within these fields of international relations inter-
> dependence has taken the place of independence,
> and the right of arbitrary decision has been def-
> initely renounced. On the other hand, states con-
> tinue to remain free agents in respect to other
> matters which remain outside the law. No obliga-
> tion can be imposed upon them, by whatever
> majority of the international community, against
> their individual wills. Each remains the guardian
> of its own interests, and the ultimate arbiter of its
> own claims. Sovereignty is here seen in its purest
> form, as a theoretical position of legal isolation
> from which the state can be brought to emerge
> only by its voluntary acts.[34]

In a footnote to this passage, the author adds the following
pertinent remark:

> That the term [sovereignty] as generally used
> in international relations is open to serious objec-

[34] Fenwick, Charles G., *International Law*, New York: Century,
1924, pp. 44-46.

tion has been long pointed out by scholars. The fact, however, that it is still in official as well as general use makes it impossible to omit reference to it.[35]

This is the subjective and voluntaristic doctrine of unrestricted sovereignty which Butler characterizes as "unsound and dangerous" and which Jenks calls "one of the greatest stumbling-blocks in the path of international progress."

In direct contrast to this theory of sovereignty is the objective Thomistic concept of the public civil power of the state, based on the nature of man and the common good. This public political power is an essential requisite for the state, for, as St. Thomas says, "if, therefore, it is natural for man to live in the society of many, it is necessary that there exist among men some means by which the group may be governed."[36] Francis of Vitoria echoes the teaching of the Master when he writes: "If councils and assemblies of men are necessary to the security of mortals, it is also true that no society can continue to exist without some force and power to govern and provide for it; the use and the utility of public power, and of the community, and of society are absolutely the same."[37] Vitoria's definition of this public power is characteristically clear and succinct: "Public power is the faculty, authority, or right to govern the civil State."[38]

This public power of the state is derived from natural law, and, consequently, comes ultimately from God, "since God is the sole author of natural law."[39] According to the Thomistic concept, this public power, coming ultimately

[35] *Ibid.*, p. 46, note 1.
[36] Si ergo naturale est homini quod in societate multorum vivat, necesse est in hominibus esse per quod multitudo regatur.—*De Reg. Prin.*, Lib. I, cap. 1.
[37] *De Potestate Civili*, 191.
[38] *Ibid.*, 201.
[39] *Ibid.*, 192; cf. St. Thomas, *Expositio in Epistolam ad Romanos*, cap. XIII, lect. 1.

from God through the natural law, resides immediately in the whole social body or the people of the state. As has been remarked previously, St. Thomas, even though he does not expressly state this view as his own in so many words, yet gives an indication of it in his treatise on law.[40] But Vitoria is very explicit on this important point.

> The State, then, possesses this power by divine disposition; but the material cause in which, by natural and divine law, power of its kind resides, is the State itself, which by its very nature is competent to govern and administer itself, and to order all its powers for the common good. The proof of this fact is as follows; since by natural and divine law there must be a power for the government of the State, and since—if common, positive, and human laws are laid aside—there is no reason for depositing that power in one person rather than in another; it necessarily follows that the community is self-sufficing and that it has the power to govern itself.[41]

This power, however, must be held and exercised by certain persons who are designated as rulers, and who constitute the government of the state: "since the State possesses power over its own parts, and since this power cannot be exercised by the multitude (which could not conveniently make laws and issue edicts, settle disputes and punish transgressors), it has therefore been necessary that the administration of the State should be entrusted to the care

[40] Ordinare autem aliquid in bonum commune est vel totius multitudinis, vel alicuius gerentis vicem totius multitudinis. Et ideo condere legem vel pertinet ad totam multitudinem, vel pertinet ad personam publicam quae totius multitudinis curam habet.—*Summa Theol.*, I, II, q. 90, a. 3.

Si enim sit libera multitudo, quae possit sibi legem facere, plus est consensus totius multitudinis ad aliquid observandum, quod consuetudo manifestat, quam auctoritas Principis, qui non habet potestatem condendi legem, nisi inquantum gerit personam multitudinis; unde licet singulae personae non possint condere legem, tamen totus populus condere legem potest.—*Ibid.*, I, II, q. 97, a. 3, ad 3.

[41] *De Potestate Civili*, 193.

of some person or persons (and it matters not whether this power is entrusted to one or to many) ."[42]

This is sufficient as an indication of the necessity, nature, and origin of the political power of the state according to the Thomistic doctrine. Our concern here is principally with the extent of this power, as well as its limitations, within the state (internal sovereignty), and especially in the relations of the state with other states (external sovereignty).

It is the concept of the common good which furnishes the key to the solution of the problem regarding the extent of the political power of the state. Herein lies the soundness and objectivity of the Thomistic doctrine. It is to achieve the common good that political power is required in the first place. It is likewise the common good which determines the scope of this power: it should be neither excessive nor deficient, but proportionate to the requirements of the common good. As far as the limitations on the power of the state is concerned, these are already implied in the proper understanding of the common good itself. In fact, in the Thomistic concept, there is much less need of insisting on the limitations on the state's power than in the modern concept of sovereignty. In the latter concept, the rights of individuals are too often regarded as retrenchments of state power, as rights wrested from an all-powerful state through the imposition of constitutional restrictions on that power. The Thomistic approach is more positive: civil power or authority is not merely limited, but is positively ordered to the end of the state, not to the particular good of those who exercise that power, but to the common good of all the members of the state.[43] Consequently, every act of public power

[42] *Ibid.*, 196.

[43] L'autorité n'est donc point seulement limitée, mais positivement ordonnée à un but, et ce but est le bien, non de son dépositaire, mais de la multitude; tout "détournement de pouvoir"—cette formule est d'usage au Conseil d'État, touchant la compétence des fonctionnaires— entraîne nullité.—Renard, R. G., "Thomisme et droit social," *Revue des Sciences philosophiques et theologiques*, vol. XXIII, 1934, p. 66.

which is contrary to the common good is an abuse, not a just and legitimate manifestation of that power.[44] And since the common good must be interpreted in the light of the general Thomistic doctrine regarding the end of man, it is essential to the very notion of that common good that the rights of the individuals derived from natural and divine positive law be safeguarded; hence, the natural law and divine positive law impose certain restrictions on the state's power. Yet not only these, but the very notion of the common good itself, viewed from the negative side, constitutes a limitation on the power of the state. Viewed in a positive manner, however, which is the more genuinely Thomistic approach, the state has power to direct and regulate the activities of its citizens in whatever concerns the common good of all. The measure of the state's power is, therefore, the common good.

So much for the Thomistic notion of the state's power and jurisdiction over its own citizens; but the question of the extent of the state's power in its relations with other states still remains to be discussed. As we have seen, the modern concept of the state's external sovereignty tends to be voluntaristic and absolute; it acknowledges no superior, personal or institutional, whose decisions in international matters must be accepted; the only decisions and restrictions which have any effect are those which are voluntarily agreed to and accepted, the state thus retaining full freedom as the final arbiter in all matters concerning its relations with other states. How does this doctrine of external sovereignty compare with the Thomistic concept?

In the first place, there is nothing in the Thomistic doctrine which makes the absence of a superior authority an essential characteristic of true sovereignty. What is essential to genuine sovereignty in the Thomistic sense is that the state constitute a complete organism having within itself the power of self-government. According to Vitoria, a sovereign is a ruler of a perfect state, and, as we have seen al-

[44] *Summa Theol.*, II, II, q. 104, a. 6, ad 3.

ready, he defines a perfect state as a community which is not part of another state, but has its own internal governmental organization.[45]   As we have also seen in this same connection, Vitoria expressly concedes that perfect states— sovereign states in the Thomistic sense—can have a superior authority, whether this be for several states,[46] for the states of Christendom,[47] or for all the states of the world.[48]   As a matter of fact, Vitoria held that there actually exists, even prior to any explicit organization of a society of states, an authority superior to the individual states which the states are bound to recognize in matters comprising the "rules of international law": this is "the authority of the whole world"—"the world as a whole, being in a way one single State."[49]   According to the Thomistic doctrine, therefore, the recognition and acceptance of a superior political authority, such as the authority of the society of states, does not conflict with the genuine notion of state sovereignty as the power of self-government.

Secondly, the notion of the universal common good, which forms the basis of the whole Thomistic international doctrine, even postulates the necessity and existence of an authority superior to the individual states in matters pertaining to the common good of all states as a whole. As has been shown in the preceding chapter, there is a hierarchy of common goods in the natural order, coresponding to which is a hierarchy of societies, each having its own proper authority;   culminating this hierarchy is the society of states with its universal common good, to which the common good of the various states is subordinate, just as the particular good of the individual is subordinate to the common good of the state, and with an authority which is superior to that of the individual states in matters pertaining to this universal common good.

[45] Vitoria, *De Jure Belli*, 425.
[46] *De Jure Belli*, 426.
[47] *De Potestate Civili*, 204.
[48] *Ibid.*, 206.
[49] *Ibid.*, 219.

This concept of an authortiy superior to that of the individual states in matters relating to the common good of all the states in their relations with one another, while it strips the state of certain absolutistic prerogatives to which it has no rightful claim, in no way impairs the genuine internal sovereignty of the state. As a self-governing community, each state has its own proper end and function to perform in looking after the common good of its own members; for this reason, the state, as a moral person, has certain fundamental rights, such as the right to existence, self-preservation and defense, the right of equality (not mathematical, but a moral equality based on identity of end), and the right to promote its own legitimate interests and common welfare.[50] These rights are natural to the state, being intimately bound up with the necessity of the state and the reason for its very existence; these fundamental rights and the power to maintain them are so natural and necessary to the state that the state cannot renounce them without at the same time renouncing its very existence as a "perfect state," in Vitoria's sense of the term.[51]

The very mention of the state's power to defend its fundamental rights raises at once the question of waging war, the ultimate expression of the state's external sovereignty. There is no need here of going into detail regarding the Scholastic doctrine on war.[52] The question will be touched only in its relation to the problem of the external sovereignty of the state.

In a brief article on war in the *Summa Theologica*, St. Thomas lays down the general principle that war is per-

[50] *A Code of International Ethics*, pp. 23-29, 40-44.

[51] *De Potestate Civili*, 201; *De Jure Belli*, 425-426.

[52] For a treatment of this question see Ryan, John K., *Modern War and Basic Ethics*, Milwaukee: Bruce Publishing Co., 1940; Stratmann, Franziskus, *The Church and War*, London: Sheed and Ward, 1928; Vann, Gerald, *Morality and War*, London: Burns Oates and Washbourne, 1939. For an historical treatment of the subject see Regout, Robert, *La doctrine de la guerre juste*, Paris: A. Pedone, 1935; also Vanderpol, A., *La doctrine scolastique du droit de guerre*, Paris: A. Pedone, 1925.

missible only if necessary "for the defense of the state and for the common good" (the latter could include non-defensive warfare under certain circumstances, such as righting a wrong done to the state). For a state to have recourse to war licitly, three conditions are required: a just cause, a right intention, and proper authority.[53] Underlying these three conditions is the general Scholastic doctrine regarding the use of physical force: war, whether defensive or justly aggressive is licit only if necessary, after other means have been attempted but failed, as the last resort against an actual evil.[54]

Although St. Thomas simply mentions that the proper authority for waging war is not that of a private person, but of a public person who holds and exercises the power of the state, Vitoria discusses this question much more in detail in his *Relectio de Jure Belli*. According to him every perfect state (in the sense of a complete, self-governing community) has the right and authority to wage war: "Such a State, then, or the prince thereof, has authority to declare war, and no one else." He concedes this right to perfect states even though they have a superior lord over them, "for (as has been said) a State ought to be self-sufficient, and this it would not be, if it had not the faculty in question."[55] This seems to contradict what has been said regarding the Thomistic doctrine (which is also Vitoria's) concerning the extent of the state's power, and to make Vitoria a champion of unlimited state sovereignty in interstate relations. That this is not the case will be readily

---

[53] Bellum pro defensione reipublicae, et pro bono communi ab eo cui regionis administratio commissa est, indictum, si recta intentione geratur, nullum peccatum est; secus autem bellare illicitum est. ... Ad hoc quod aliquod bellum sit justum, tria requiruntur. Primo quidem auctoritas principis, cujus mandato bellum est gerendum. ... Secundo requiritur causa justa; ut scilicet illi qui impugnantur, propter aliquam culpam impugnationem mereantur. ... Tertio requiritur ut sit intentio bellantium recta; qua scilicet intenditur vel ut bonum promoveatur, vel ut malum vitetur.—*Summa Theol.*, II, II, q. 40, a. 1.

[54] Ryan, John K., *Modern War and Basic Ethics*, p. 40.

[55] *De Jure Belli*, 426.

seen by looking at Vitoria's views on this question as a whole.

Vitoria explains the state's authority and competence to wage war in terms of a juridical process. In the absence of any competent court of judgment to decide disputes between states and to enforce its decisions, rulers of perfect states, whose rights have been violated and who have justice on their side, are regarded as judges in matters pertaining to war.[56] Furthermore, in the absence of a higher coercive power to right wrongs received—which is the "single and only just cause for commencing a war"[57]—the ruler who has this just cause is regarded as having jurisdiction over those from whom the wrong has been received, and consequently has authority to make good this wrong, even by the physical force of warfare, if necessary.[58]   Dr. Scott thus summarizes Vitoria's views on this point:

> The prince is therefore in fact, if not in form, a judge.
> The doctrine of Francisco de Vitoria is in its entirety that of a judicial system for the entire world, with the princes or sovereign authorities of the States as judges of the violation of rights under the law of nations until there should be a court between, and therefore above, the nations. Hence it is that Vitoria's prince may redress rights and punish wrongs just as may a judge of civil or criminal jurisdiction.... In like manner, and on an international scale, the prince is the executor of the judgment which he has rendered. And finally, this judgeship—if we may so term it—was not the exclusive right of one State but of any and all States against which a wrong had been committed.[59]

The solution of the problem regarding the authority and right of states to wage war, as the necessary means of self-

[56] *Ibid.*, 431.
[57] *Ibid.*, 429.
[58] *Ibid.*, 429-431.
[59] Scott, James Brown, *The Spanish Origin of International Law, Part I: Francisco de Victoria and his Law of Nations*, pp. 210-211.

defense or of righting wrongs received, does not lie in the
outright denial of that right to the state, but rather in the
removal of the necessity of the states to resort to this right
and authority. This necessity can be removed only if there
exists a society of states with competent judicial and
coercive authority, and if the states fulfill their obligation
of recognizing this authority, once legitimately constituted,
and abiding by its decisions: both conditions are necessary.
Under such an organization proper channels would be provided for the settlement of disputes between states, for the
protection of states against the encroachments of other
states, and for righting of wrongs received through violation of the states' legitimate rights. Yet it must be added
that even under such an organization, the individual self-
governing member states do not cede or lose the fundamental rights which they have by nature nor the authority
and moral power of defending these rights; consequently,
should the authority of the society of states fail to provide
the individual member state with adequate protection and
assurances of justice, the individual state, confronted with
the necessity of defending itself by resort to physical force,
would not have to retrieve its right and authority of waging
war, but would *ipso facto* be in the position to exercise the
right which it possessed all along. In this connection, a
passage in *A Code of International Ethics* dealing with the
question of disarmament, expressive of the realistic approach to this problem, is apropos.

> Failing certain and effective guarantees, who can
> reasonably blame any Power exposed to threats of
> aggression, for refusing to think of any reductions
> in its means of defence?
>
> Certain utopian theorists, by arbitrarily trans-
> posing the terms of the problem, have vainly
> thought it was sufficient to institute general dis-
> armament, after having led all States to accept
> compulsory arbitration, in order to achieve perfect
> security. To their trilogy, *arbitration, disarma-
> ment, security,* sound realism opposes a more ra-
> tional formula *arbitration, security, disarmament.*

> Nations can only disarm if their security is guaranteed against any power which, in violation of its agreements, would refuse to have recourse to arbitration or submit to its decisions. So long as this security does not come under any collective guarantee, each State will have to provide its own means of defence.[60]

That the Vitorian (and the Thomistic) theory regarding the authority of the state to wage war is not opposed to the objective Thomistic doctrine of state sovereignty, but on the contrary is incompatible with the modern subjective doctrine of sovereignty, is thus indicated by Dr. Scott.

> The conception of Victoria in all its parts looks to a permanent international organization, with the institution of a permanent international judiciary. It is not improper to observe that the world of our day seems not yet to have grasped the full significance and meaning of the Spanish Dominican's doctrine. Modern nations, to be sure, have long been accustomed to act as judges in controversies affecting them; but too often they have insisted, and still insist, on this as their peculiar and exclusive right, stubbornly maintaining that in all disputes which concern their interests they themselves, even if their cause be the most dubious, are the sole judges competent to enter judgement. Victoria's view was that each and every ruler had the power of a judge only if his cause were just, and that his support of an unjust cause stripped him at once, so far as international law was concerned, of any power to pass on the right or wrong of the controversy. The simple truth is that the Victorian conception is entirely incompatible with the doctrine of sovereignty, by which, in its baldest form, each so-called sovereign nation claims the absolute right to do as it pleases in so far as its strength permits, without reference to the rights of any other nation or to the international community and its rules.[61]

[60] *A Code of International Ethics*, p. 114.
[61] Scott, James Brown, *The Spanish Origin of International Law, Part I: Francisco de Victoria and his Law of Nations*, pp. 211-212.

A final point must be mentioned dealing with the relation of the individual states to the society of states as a whole, with special reference to the question of sovereignty. How is the sovereignty of the individual states affected by their collective organization into a society of states? This, of course, has reference to external authority, since, as has been mentioned previously, internal sovereignty, understood in the Thomistic sense, remains intact under such an organization. In the opinion of many people any and every restriction on the absolute external freedom of the state as a result of the functioning of an approved international authority is regarded as so much "sacrifice" of the state's sovereignty. Such an opinion is, consciously or unconsciously, only the manifestation of the theory of sovereignty underlying it. Granted, of course, the subjective and voluntaristic notion of state sovereignty in which the state claims complete freedom of action in its external affairs, the mutual cooperation and organization is possible only at the cost of "sacrificing" some of the sovereignty of the individual states to the authority of all the states collectively. An organization of states constructed on this notion would have a purely contractual basis in which each state agrees voluntarily to the cession of so much of its external sovereignty and unrestricted freedom of action for the purpose of achieving the collective security of all the states concerned. Such is the concept of the international community held by those who wish to retain the traditional theory of sovereignty, since "the traditional theory of sovereignty implies the complete freedom of a state from the control of any higher power claiming authority to regulate its acts; whatever rules of conduct are recognized by the state as binding upon it must be self-imposed obligations."[62]

But this is neither the sole nor the soundest approach to the problem. According to the Thomistic concept of the state and its power, or sovereignty, and of the society of states with its authority, there is no question of "sacrificing"

[62] Fenwick, *op. cit.*, p. 44.

the former to the latter, but of ordering positively each of the states towards the common good of all. Instead of the states losing, they actually gain by sharing in the peace and order implied in the common good. Although an explicit and voluntary agreement is necessary on the part of the states to actualize the community of states which exists potentially in an unorganized form in nature, and thus give it a definite organization, yet this agreement or act of organization, in the Thomistic concept, is not a mere contract, like the "social contract" of Hobbes or Rousseau, in which the states agree to give up certain rights or prerogatives to the community of states in return for the guarantee of collective security—*a quid pro quo*—without regard to any objective foundation in nature for a universal common good; this act of organization is rather, to use the expression of Father Delos, and act of "incorporation' 'by which the states become members of an organic community of states, for the society of states, like the state itself, is a genuine social organism in which the notion of the common good is the "generative idea" or motivating force.[63]

[63] These expressions are taken from a passage by Father Delos in which he offers an interesting explanation of the process through which the political power of the social body or the state is vested in the person of the ruler. For the sake of comparison the passage is here given in full.

La tradition thomiste,—et Suarez, sur ce point, lui est fidèle,— voit dans le corps social,—disons, avec sa terminologie, dans le peuple, —le titulaire naturel du pouvoir public. Mais quelle est la nature juridique de l'acte par lequel la nation use de sa liberté pour se donner des chefs commis au soin de ses intérêts?

L'on sait la réponse que donne à cette question la conception institutionnelle et organique de l'État. La collation du pouvoir s'analyse en un double mouvement: d'une part, l'acte de l'individu qui devient le fonctionnaire, l'organe, le chef,—et d'autre part, l'acte du corps social qui nomme ou accepte ses gouvernants. Il ya donc manifestation d'une double volonté, et un accord s'établit entre elles. Mais de quelle nature est-il?

Du côté du souverain nommé,—ou du fonctionnaire,—il y a une *adhésion* au Bien social de la Communauté. Le fait d'accepter ou de briguer la fonction, le fait même de se l'approprier, se ramènent à

In the following paragraphs Georges Renard shows the fundamental difference between the concept of international law, and consequently of an international society, which is based on the contractual theory of society and the doctrine of unlimited state sovereignty, and one which is based objectively on the Thomistic notion of order and the common good.

> There are two basic conceptions of the law of nations. The first, inspired by Jean Jacques Rousseau and the "Social Contract," lays down that the state of nature among nations is independence. Being independent they then bind themselves to each other by treaties. On the one hand we have the independence and equality of States, and, on the other, respect for engagements entered into by States; all international law is governed by these two theses and this is the classic conception of it, whereby it is built up without reference to any objective principle and becomes a law not of subordination but of coordination only....
>
> The purely contractual conception of international law springs from a system of philosophy according to which sovereignty is an absolute unlimited power which resides in its fullest development in the State. If this is so, all liberty, individual and corporate, is merely an uncertain con-

---

une prise en charge du Bien commun. Le futur fonctionnaire en fait, assure-t-il, l'objet et la fin de son activité: c'est une mise en service de sa personne, au bénéfice du Bien commun.

Du côté du groupe, il y a *adhésion*—implicite ou explicite—à la personne du dépositaire de l'autorité, parce qu'en elle il voit l'organe adapté de son Bien, le pourvoyeur efficace, ou du moins possible, du Bien commun dont il est en quête.

Il n'y a donc rien ici d'un "contrat" au sens du droit privé. Il n'y a qu'un phénomène d'*adhésion*, dominée par l'*idée* d'un Bien social objectif à procurer. Ainsi s'opère une *incorporation*. Le mot est exact: car la société est un corps, à qui le Bien commun fournit l'idée-génératrice et le bien. Le nouveau fonctionnaire s'incorpore le bien commun qu'il fait sien, le corps social s'incorpore la personne du fonctionnaire; celui-ci devient organe du groupe et du Bien commun. —Delos, J. T., Review of Heinrich Rommen, *Die Staatslehre des Franz Suarez, S. J., Bulletin Thomiste*, VI, no. 2, March 1929, pp. 493-494.

cession which the State can revoke at any time and
all authority, even that of the father of the family,
is delegated by the State at its discretion.   No-
body has the right to look over the wall which
separates States from each other.

In actual fact, sociability is not accidental or
subordinate either as between individuals or nations, and Rousseau was wrong in thinking so.
There is a natural society between nations and
therefore a juridical system of which treaties are,
and ought to be, only an adaptation to the infinite
variety of historical conditions.   It is from their
conformity with the pre-existent natural law and
from their fitness to make it work in harmony with
the circumstances of the times that treaties derive
their binding force.   Treaties are not the source of
international law;   but it is from this law that
they derive their legal validity.   International law
does not proceed from treaties but rules them. . . .
Order and the common good are the basis of international law.   To them sovereignty and freedom must not be sacrificed but subjected.   This
is the Christian conception of the law of nations
founded   on   the   philosophy   of   St.   Thomas
Aquinas.[64]

To sum up this discussion regarding the relation of the
individual states to the society of states: on the one hand,
each individual member state has specific functions to perform towards its citizens for which it requires the power
to govern itself without undue interference from any outside power, and, consequently, each state is a "perfect
society" and a "sovereign state" in the Thomistic sense as
explained above, but not, however, in the absolute and unlimited sense of the terms;   on the other hand, each of
these member states has certain positive functions to perform towards the society of states as a whole, which func-

[64] Renard, Georges, "Les fondements philosophiques du droit international," in *Les grandes activités de la Société des Nations devant la
pensée Chretienne*, Paris: Editions Spes, 1932.   English translation
from Eppstein, *The Catholic Tradition of the Law of Nations*, pp.
308-309.

tions are at the same time moral obligations, such as the recognition and acceptance of the legitimately constituted international authority and positive cooperation in promoting the universal common good of all the states. Since these obligations have been sufficiently indicated in the preceding chapter, there is no need of repeating them here. But there still remains to be considered briefly the relation of the society of states to the individual member states.

II.   The Society of States in Relation to the Individual States.

There are also two aspects under which the society of states can be considered in relation to the individual member states: under the positive aspect of the extent of its powers and functions and negatively from the viewpoint of the limitations on these same powers and functions. Both of these have already been treated to some extent. The positive aspect has been indicated in the preceding chapter under the section on "The Objective Requirements in an Organized Society of States," where it was shown that for the effective organization of such a society and the fulfillment of its purpose three types of functions and corresponding powers are essential: judicial, legislative, and coercive. And in the present chapter the limitations on these functions and powers have by implication been indicated in discussing the rights, functions, and powers of the individual state as a "perfect society" and "sovereign state" in the Thomistic conception of these terms. Hence it will suffice to connect the two points of view without going into any lengthy details concerning them.

As a general norm for both the extent and the limitations of the functions and powers of the society of states, no sounder principle can be found than that enunciated by Pope Pius XI, which he calls an "unshaken and unchangeable fundamental principle of social philosophy." Although this principle is laid down by Pope Pius in connection with the state's relation to subordinate social and economic groups, yet the principle itself is applicable with equal force to the functions of the society of states in relation to the various member states. Pope Pius writes:

> ... it is an injustice, a grave evil and a disturbance of right order for a larger and higher organization to arrogate to itself functions which can be performed efficiently by smaller and lower bodies. This is a fundamental principle of social philosophy, unshaken and unchangeable and it retains its full truth today. Of its very nature the true aim of all social activity should be to help the individual members of the social body, but never to destroy or absorb them.[65]

This "fundamental principle of social philosophy" is a Thomistic principle derived from the Thomistic concept of the organic and hierarchical structure of society.[66] According to this concept the total, integral social and political order is composed of various groups, one subordinate to the other, each having its own common good to attain and specific functions to perform. It is this social order which is disturbed when the specific functions of one group are arrogated or absorbed by another group, as, for example, when the state attempts to absorb the functions of the family. Applied to the political order, there are certain functions which the state has to perform towards its own citizens, which follow from the very nature and purpose of the state; these functions are proper to the state and it would be a "disturbance of right order" for the international society to arrogate them to itself or even to interfere with them so long as they are being properly performed by the state itself. While this higher society may and should recommend and lend assistance to the state in the performance of its internal functions in case of need, (and, in the event that the state should fail seriously to perform its functions, thereby upsetting the social order, this higher

---

[65] Pope Pius XI, Encyclical Letter *Quadragesimo Anno.*

[66] cf. *Summa Theol,* I, II, q. 21, a. 3; II, II, q. 58, a. 7, ad 2; III, q. 8, a. 1, ad 2.

society should intervene for the common good of the state itself and for the universal common good of all the states), yet the international society should not take over these functions of the state, for "of its very nature the true aim of all social activity should be to help the individual members of the social body, but never to destroy or absorb them."[67] There are other functions, however, which involve relations between states and which pertain to the common good of all the states collectively: these are the functions which are proper to the society of states.

Among the specific functions proper to the society of states, those are of special importance which involve the exercise of legislative authority. The judicial and coercive functions of the society are to a great extent conditioned by its legislative functions, inasmuch as judicial decisions in interstate matters are made according to the norms of law, natural and positive, regulating relations between states, and the coercive functions concern the enforcement of these decisions and laws. Since, therefore, the extent of the judicial and coercive functions of the society of states is largely determined by the scope of the society's legislative functions, the latter should be given more detailed consideration. The following passage from *The World Society* contains the recommendations of The Catholic Association for International Peace on this point, which are offered here on their own merit.

> A Commonwealth of Nations without legislative functions and legislative organization would be lacking in the essential quality of an international authority. Deprived of legislative powers, it could be little more than an advisory body having some feeble authority to warn and admonish.
>
> What legislative functions might be possessed by a Commonwealth of Nations in order that it may have competent political authority to direct the nations of the world towards an international common good? In the section on the economics of world society we concluded that some international

[67] Pope Pius XI, Encyclical Letter *Quadragesimo Anno.*

agency should have the power to regulate, and even sometimes to control international markets in raw materials, manufactured and agricultural goods and services and the multiple forms of international finance.... International control over colonial areas after the type of the Mandates system seems necessary. International legislation could co-ordinate and advance national labor laws.

In addition to an international economic authority the legislative functions of a Commonwealth of Nations might be used to encourage, promote, and assist in the enforcement of national minority treaties....

A third group of powers which might be conferred upon the legislature of the world society would deal with the enforcement of peace. The imposition of economic sanctions, the employment of an international police force, and the power to reduce armaments might be included among the lawmaking functions of the world Commonwealth.

The progress of world communication and transportation as well as the promotion of public health, safety, and morals and the advancement of intellectual and cultural co-operation depend upon the continuance and the fortification of existing agencies brought together to work out programs of action. Some of these matters are well regulated by bilateral or multilateral treaties; others of them require the co-operation of the whole body of nations.[68]

The last sentence is very significant; it recalls Pope Pius' fundamental and important principle that "functions which can be performed efficiently by smaller and lower bodies" should not be absorbed by a "larger and higher organization."

Consequently, the notion of a World State, a single superstate, reaching down to all individual men and the activities of their daily lives, is foreign to the Thomistic concept of the social and political order. Foreign, too, is the notion of a universal stateless society, a notion of Marxist origin, which

[68] *The World Society,* pp. 40-41.

in reality could become only a huge state, obliterating state
boundaries, and attempting to perform the functions (according to Marxist principles, of course) which in the
natural social order are performed by the individual state.
In fact, any concept of a super-state absorbing individual
states and their functions, whether dominated by the idea of
power, race, nation, class, or cultural superiority, is the
very antithesis of the Thomistic conception of social and
political order. For Thomism does not conceive this social
and political order as a horizontal "leveling" of all men to
a single universal social and political stratum; rather it
conceives it as an harmonious integration of the various
social and political groups, each having its specific end and
functions, into a complete, organic, hierarchical socio-politi-
cal structure. Many persons fear the creation of a commonwealth or society of states lest it develop into a vast super-
state, like the dreaded "Leviathan" of Hobbes, but these
fears can have no foundation in the Thomistic conception of
the political order.

The principle of respect for subordinate social groups
applies also to national groups—nations, in the sense of
racial and cultural groups, rather than in the sense of
political communities or states. These national groups are
natural to man and have certain specific functions to perform in the development of man's nature. "The nation,
like the State, is a community grounded in human nature;
the values of nationality are necessary to the full development of man's personality."[69] These natural racial and cultural groups are the gift of nature and its Creator for the
enrichment of the human race and its civilization. The sup-
pression or absorption of these national groups would, consequently, be also a "disturbance of right order."

> On the other hand, it is a fact, willed by the
> Author of nature Himself, that humanity, in itself
> a unity, should be diversified in individuals and
> societies according to heredity, natural and social

---

[69] Delos, J. T., "Political Causes of International Disorder," in *The
Foundations of International Order*, p. 42.

surroundings, education and customs. The traits
and characteristics which constitute a nationality
are therefore natural values which each national
group has the right to maintain, enrich and defend
against any attempt at assimilation or absorption.[70]

There are two extremes to be avoided on this point. The
one extreme exalts the nation with its culture and political
power into an absolute, to which the cultural values of other
nations must be sacrificed; this is an "exaggerated nationalism" which is incompatible with any true international society. The other extreme is an "excessive internationalism" which aims at the abolition of all nationalities
and cultural differences—which is but another phase of the
Marxist "classless society." The proper evaluation of
national groups lies betwen these two extremes: they have
the right to exist, but not as absolute values; they have
their proper place and functions in the social hierarchy;
as such they should be safeguarded and assisted, not de-
stroyed or absorbed by the international society of states.
This is the Thomistic solution. Herein, too, lies the basis
for real harmony between genuine nationalism or patriotism
and true internationalism, as distinguished from the exaggerated nationalism and excessive internationalism described above. Both of these imply duties for the individual
human person—duties which are not contradictory, but complementary. By patriotism (or nationalism, in this sense
of the term) man has certain duties towards his own country: a duty of love and devotion towards his native land,
in which he was born, and its people, among whom he was
brought up and educated;[71] a duty also of social justice
towards his country as the political community or state
promoting the common good of himself and his fellow citizens. By reason of true internationalism the individual
human person also has certain duties—duties which are dis-
charged directly by cherishing a spirit of love and appre-

[70] *A Code of International Ethics,* p. 126.
[71] *Summa Theol.,* II, II, q. 101, a. 1.

ciation for the peoples of other countries as members of the human family, and indirectly by contributing through the state to the international common good. According to Thomistic social and political philosophy, there is a real harmony, not an antagonism, between genuine nationalism and true internationalism.

CONCLUSION

In the preface to this dissertation was quoted the statement of Pope Pius XI indicating the significance of the doctrine of St. Thomas as the basis for a true international society. There Pope Pius expressly mentioned that St. Thomas treats of social and political subjects not only from the natural order, but from the supernatural order as well. In the same preface it was noted that the particular approach to the problem of international society followed in these pages would be that of philosophy, and specifically of Thomistic philosophy. For this reason the concept of an international society based on right reason and the natural law has been emphasized; yet, as was also mentioned at the very outset, this approach does not imply any denial or undervaluation of the supernatural; rather, it has been acknowledged throughout that the supernatural order rises above and supplements the natural order. Before closing this treatise, therefore, the important contribution of the principles of supernatural revealed religion to international order and the formation of international society will be indicated, but only briefly, for a lengthy development is beyond the scope of this work. By supernatural revealed religion is meant the Christian Religion as handed down through nineteen centuries by the Church of Christ, the Catholic Church.

The successor of Pius XI as the Head of Christendom, Pius XII, gives expression to the need of the principles of revealed religion to vivify and supplement the principles of the natural law: "the new order of the world, of national and international life, ... must rest on the unshakable foundation, on the solid rock of natural law and Divine Revelation."[1] Let us then briefly summarize the chief points in the outline of a society of states based upon principles of the natural order, and see how the principles of the super-

---

[1] Pope Pius XII, Encyclical Letter *Summi Pontificatus.*

natural order, of revealed Christian teaching, animate, strengthen, and supplement each.

1. In the natural order the existence of a universal society embracing all men and all peoples is postulated by the nature of man and his natural social tendencies. Pope Pius XII, while fully admitting the natural unity of the human race, regards the unity of this race from the supernatural point of view as "a marvelous vision, which makes us see the human race in the unity of one common origin in God, 'one God and Father of all, Who is above all, and through all, and in us all' (Ephesians iv, 6)." And after enumerating the various supernatural factors making for human unity, he concludes: "These are supernatural truths which form a solid basis and the strongest possible bond of a union, that is reinforced by the law of God and of our Divine Redeemer, from Whom all receive salvation 'for the edifying of the Body of Christ: until we all meet into the unity of faith, and of the knowledge of the Son of God, unto a perfect man, unto the measure of the age of the fulness of Christ' (Ephesians, iv, 12, 13)."[2]

2. There exists a universal common good of all men and all peoples; it is the recognition of this common good which provides the motivating impulse for the formation of a true society of states. Yet this universal common good itself cannot be fully appreciated without taking into account the final end of man, which is a "supernatural end, God Himself, to Whom all should tend."[3] Furthermore, as we have seen, this universal common good implies order and peace among all peoples, and peace is directly and primarily the work of charity, not simply and solely natural benevolence, but supernatural charity.[4]

3. No true international society can be organized and effectively maintained without the agreement of the members on necessary fundamental principles. These are in the first instance principles of the natural order derived from the natural law. Yet the truths of Divine Revelation give

[2] *Ibid.*   [3] *Ibid.*   [4] *Summa Theol.*, II, II, q. 29, a. 3, ad 3.

solidity and stability to this natural foundation; both together constitute "the unshakable foundation" and "the solid rock of natural law and Divine Revelation."[5]

4.   The moral virtues of justice and charity are an indispensable condition for the proper functioning of an international society. Of these, charity is the distinctive Christian virtue; through it the love of man for his fellow man is based not simply on likeness of nature, but especially on likeness through creation by God and through our common Redemption by Jesus Christ, by reason of which men become the adopted sons of a common Father and brothers one of another. Christian charity, therefore, is universal in scope, extending to all men of all nations.

5.   Authority is an essential requisite for an international society. This authority—judicial, legislative, and coercive—is required by the very nature of man and society, and is therefore based on and derived from the natural law. But supernatural revelation ennobles this authority and strengthens its binding power through its doctrine concerning the Creator of nature from Whom all authority is derived, "for there exists no authority except from God." (Romans xiii, 1.)

6.   Individual states are related to the society of states as parts to the whole, not physically but morally, as members of a moral organism. Both the members individually and the society as a whole have specific ends and functions which are not to be confused or absorbed, one by another. These two elements of the integral political order—individual member states and the society as a whole—give rise respectively to the duties of patriotism and internationalism in the true sense of the terms. Both of these are recognized, safeguarded, and encouraged as mutually compatible by the principles of Christianity. As Pope Pius says:

> Nor is there any fear lest the consciousness of universal brotherhood aroused by the teaching of Christianity, and the spirit which it inspires, be in

[5] Pope Pius XII, Encyclical Letter *Summi Pontificatus.*

contrast with the love of traditions or the glories
of one's fatherland, or impede the progress of
prosperity or legitimate interests. For that same
Christianity teaches that in the exercise of charity
we must follow a God-given order, yielding the
place of honor in our affections and good works to
those who are bound to us by special ties. Nay, the
Divine Master Himself gave an example of this
preference for His Own country and fatherland,
as He wept over the coming destruction of the Holy
City. But legitimate and well-ordered love of our
native country should not make us close our eyes to
the all-embracing nature of Christian charity,
which calls for consideration of others and of their
interests in the pacifying light of love.[6]

From this it is evident that the Christian Religion with
its revealed truths and moral teaching is an exceedingly
important and vital force in promoting peaceful and order-
ly relations between men and nations. Even if the philosopher, political theorist, or practical statesman would not
accept this Religion as divinely revealed, he is nevertheless
forced to acknowledge its importance as a powerful
sociological factor making for unity among men and nations.
So powerful, in fact, is this force of Christianity that some
regard it as the sole basis for international order and a community of states. According to these, the only feasible and
workable community of states is that which is composed
exclusively of peoples who have inherited the Christian
tradition, who accept Christian principles, at least nominally, and are therefore entitled to be called Christian states.
This is the conclusion of Ross J. S. Hoffman in his recent
book, *The Great Republic,* after making a survey of attempts
to form a community of states since the beginning of the
Christian era.[7]

It is true, as has also been shown in the first chapter of
this treatise, that the earlier attempts at international

[6] Pope Pius XII, *Summi Pontificatus.*

[7] Hoffman, Ross J. F., *The Great Republic,* New York: Sheed and
Ward, 1942, pp. 153-4.

organization were confined to Christian states. Although certain proposals offered since the sixteenth century have suggested the inclusion of non-Christian states into the community of states, yet it was not until recent times that such states were actually included under the League of Nations. But what of the present and the future? Should the international community be limited to those states which possess the common Christian heritage and culture and which can be designated as Christian States in the wide sense; or should it be universal and embrace all states, Christian and non-Christian, so long as they are capable of active membership by reason of sufficient political and cultural development? In other words, the question resolves itself to this: can there be a society of states for which the principles of the natural law serve as a basis, or must such a society be based only on Christian principles and embrace only Christian states? The answer is that it is not necessary to set up such a dilemma, for there is no contradition between the natural and the Christian basis. The supernatural ennobles the natural, but does not contradict or destroy it. There is a natural basis in the rational and social nature of man and in the natural law for a genuine international community. This has been the principal thesis of this treatise. But the supernatural, Christian basis strengthens and solidifies the natural basis. The one is good, but the other is better. It would certainly be the ideal if all states throughout the world would be Christian states, guided really, not merely nominally, by Christian principles, and if these states were organized into a community of states founded on Christian teaching. But this is far from a reality at the present time. What then? Granted the need of a community of states—and who can reasonably deny it?—there are the two alternatives: a community of (traditionally) Christian states, or a universal society embracing all states and based, at least, on the principles of the natural law.

As to the former, much can be said of the common traditional, historical, and cultural ties which tend to create a consciousness of unity and to bind these states together—ties which flow originally from the common religion of Christianity, even though many of the people and the governments of these states reject, at least in practice if not always in theory, the very teachings of this common, unifying Religion. On the other hand, the organization of a community of states expressly including some and explicitly excluding other states, on the basis of a common religious heritage, would, it seems, create antagonisms between the Christian and the non-Christian communities of states, which would mean the transfer of inter-state conflicts to the more comprehensive plane of inter-community, inter-empire, or inter-continental antagonisms. Such conflicts could hardly be obviated considering the very close ties of economic interdependence existing even now between the states of these two groups. As a matter of fact, the vast majority of the states which have been members of the League of Nations at one time or another—at least fifty out of the fifty-eight—are traditionally Christian states. Yet this fact did not of itself save the League from collapse or at least from temporary discontinuance of functions. In addition to the weaknesses within the organization of the League of Nations itself, such as the lack of adequate authority and the underlying contractual idea which attempts to compromise with the subjective, voluntaristic, notion of unlimited state sovereignty, the failure of the League was due to the failure of some of the states, also the traditionally Christian states, to observe even the obligations imposed by natural law regarding just and amicable relations between states.

On the contrary, the Popes themselves, the spiritual leaders of Christendom, have encouraged the establishment of an international society, not restricted to Christian states, but universal, embracing all states. Thus Pope Benedict XV urged "that *all* States should put aside mutual suspicion and unite in *one sole society* or rather *family of peoples*, both to guarantee their own independence and safeguard order in the civil concert of peoples."[8] Such, therefore, is the aim of Christian teaching itself, as well as of the teaching of Thomistic political philosophy. Pope Pius XII has indicated this fundamental teaching of Thomistic philosophy, as well as of Christianity, in a brief paragraph which is at once both an excellent summary and an appropriate conclusion to the present treatise.

> A disposition, in fact, of the divinely-sanctioned natural order divides the human race into social groups, nations or States, which are mutually independent in organization and in the direction of their internal life. But for all that, the human race is bound together by reciprocal ties, moral and juridical, into a great commonwealth directed to the good of all nations and ruled by special laws which protect its unity and promote its prosperity.[9]

[8] Pope Benedict XV, Encyclical Letter *Pacem Dei Munus Pulcherrimum.* (Italics mine).

[9] Pope Pius XII, Encyclical Letter *Summi Pontificatus.*

BIBLIOGRAPHY

Aquinas, St. Thomas, *Opera Omnia*, Paris: Vives Edition, 1871-1880.

――――, *Summa Theologia*. Translation by the English Dominican Fathers, London: Burns Oates and Washbourne; New York: Benziger, 1911-1922.

――――, *Summa Contra Gentiles*. Translation by the English Dominican Fathers, London: Burns Oates and Washbourne; New York: Benziger, 1923-1929.

――――, *De Regimine Principum*. Translation by Gerald B. Phelan, *On the Governance of Rulers*, Toronto: St. Michael's College, 1935; New York: Sheed and Ward, 1938.

――――, *In Libros Politicorum Expositio*.

――――, *In Decem Libros Ethicorum Expositio*.

――――, *Contra Impugnantes Dei Cultum et Religionem*.

――――, *Expositio in Evangelium S. Matthaei*.

――――, *Expositio in S. Pauli Epistolas*.

――――, *Scriptum super Libros Sententiarum*.

Aristotle, *Nichomachean Ethics*. Translation by W. D. Ross, in *The Basic Works of Aristotle*, New York: Random House, 1941.

――――, *Politics*. Translation by Benjamin Jowett, in *The Basic Works of Aristotle*, New York: Randon House, 1941.

Augustine, St., *De Civitate Dei*, Migne, *Patres Latini*, vol. 41. Translation by Marcus Dods, vol. II of "Select Library of the Nicene and Post Nicene Fathers of the Christian Church," Buffalo: The Christian Literature Co., 1887.

Barthélemy, J., "Francois de Vitoria," in *Les fondateurs du droit international*, Paris: V. Girard et E. Briere, 1904.

Batiffol and others, *L'Eglise et le droit de guerre*, Paris: Bloud et Gay, 1920.

Baupin and others, *La Société Internationale*, Paris: de Gigord, 1928.

Beales, A. C. F., *The Catholic Church and International Order*, New York: Allen Lane, 1941.

――――, *The History of Peace*, New York: Dial Press, 1931.

Beuve-Méry, Hubert, *La Theorie des pouvoirs public d'apres Francisco de Vitoria*, Paris: Editions Spes, 1928.

de la Brière, Yves, *La conception du droit international chez les theologiens catholiques*, Paris: Centre Européen de la Dotation Carnegie pour la Paix Internationale, 1930.

――――, *L'organisation internationale du monde contemporain et la Papauté Souveraine*, Paris: Editions Spes, 1927.

de la Brière, Yves et P. M. Colbach, *La Patrie et la Paix: Textes Pontificaux*, Paris: Desclée de Brouwer, 1938.

Brown, W. E., *The Achievement of the Middle Ages*, St. Louis: Herder, 1928.

Brown, Stephen J., (editor) *International Relations from a Catholic Standpoint*, Dublin: Browne and Nolan, 1932.

Bryce, James, *The Holy Roman Empire*, New York: A. L. Burt, 1886.

Cahill, Edward, *The Framework of a Christian State*, Dublin: Gill and Son, 1932.

Cajetan, Thomas de Vio, Cardinal, *Commentaria in Summam Theologicam S. Thomae Aquinatis*, in Leonine edition of the works of St. Thomas, Rome, 1882.

Carlyle, R. W. and A. J. Carlyle, *A History of Mediaeval Political Theory in the West*, 6 vols., Edinburgh: Wm. Blackwood, 1927-1936.

Cicero, Marcus Tullius, *De Finibus Bonorum et Malorum*. Translation by H. Rackham (Loeb Classical Library), New York: Macmillan, 1914.

———, *De Officiis*. Translation by W. Miller (Loeb Classical Library), New York: Macmillan, 1913.

———, *Tusculan Disputations*. Translation by J. E. King (Loeb Classical Library), New York: Putnam's, 1917.

Clonmore, Lord, *Pope Pius XI and World Peace*, New York: Dutton, 1938.

A Code of International Ethics, Oxford: Catholic Social Guild, 1940.

A Code of Social Principles, Oxford: Catholic Social Guild, 1931.

Cook, Thomas I., *History of Political Philosophy from Plato to Burke*, New York: Prentice-Hall, 1936.

Crahay, Édouard, *La politique de Saint Thomas d'Aquin*, Louvain: Institut Supérieur de Philosophie, 1896.

Dante Alighieri, *De Monarchia*. Translation by A. Henry, Boston: Houghton Mifflin, 1904.

Dawson, Christopher, *The Making of Europe*, New York: Sheed and Ward, 1938.

Delos, J. T., *La société internationale et les principes du droit public*, Paris: A. Pedone, 1929.

———, "Christian Principles and International Relations" in Brown, Stephen J., *International Relations from a Catholic Standpoint*, Dublin: Browne and Nolan, 1932.

———, "Political Causes of International Disorder" in *The Foundations of International Order*, Oxford: Catholic Social Guild, 1938.

Dempf, Alois, *Christliche Staatsphilosophie in Spanien*, Salzburg: Anton Pustet, 1937.

————, *Sacrum Imperium—Geschichte und Staatsphilosophie des Mittelalters und der politischen Renaissance*, Munich: R. Oldenbourg, 1929.

Dougherty, George V., *The Moral Basis of Social Order according to St. Thomas*, Washington: The Catholic University of America Press, 1941.

Dunning, William A., *History of Political Theories, Ancient and Medieval*, New York: Macmillan, 1927.

Eppstein, John, *The Catholic Tradition of the Law of Nations*, London: Burns Oates and Washbourne, 1935.

Eyre, Edward, *European Civilization, its Origin and Development*, New York: Oxford University Press, 1935.

Farrell, Walter, *The Natural Moral Law according to St. Thomas and Suarez*, Ditchling: St. Dominic's Press, 1930.

Fenwick, Charles G., *International Law*, New York: Century, 1924.

Figgis, John N., *Studies in Political Thought from Gerson to Grotius*, New York: Putnam's, 1907.

The Foundations of International Order, Oxford: Catholic Social Guild, 1938.

Gentili, Alberico, *De iure belli libri tres.* Translation by John C. Rolfe, in "Classics of International Law," Carnegie Endowment for International Peace, 2 vols., Oxford: At the Clarendon Press, 1933.

Gierke, Otto, *Political Theories of the Middle Age*, Cambridge: The University Press, 1922.

Grotius, Hugo, *De jure belli ac pacis libri tres.* Translation by F. W. Kelsey and others, in "Classics of International Law," Carnegie Endowment for International Peace, 2 vols., Oxford: At the Clarendon Press, 1925.

Harley, John E., *Documentary Textbook on International Relations*, Los Angeles: Suttonhouse, 1934.

Hayes, Carlton J. H., *Essays on Nationalism*, New York: Macmillan, 1933.

————, *The Historical Evolution of Modern Nationalism*, New York: Richard R. Smith, 1931.

————, "Medieval Diplomacy" in Walsh, E. A., *The History and Nature of International Relations*, New York: Macmillan, 1922.

Hearnshaw, F. J. C. (editor), *The Social and Political Ideas of some Great Mediaeval Thinkers*, London: George G. Harrap, 1923.

————, *The Social and Political Ideas of some Great Thinkers of the Sixteenth and Seventeenth Centuries*, London: George G. Harrap, 1926.

Hill, D. J., *History of Diplomacy in the International Development of Europe*, 3 vols., New York: Longmans, Green, 1905.

Hodges, Charles, *The Background of International Relations*, New York: John Wiley, 1931.

Hoffman, Ross J. S., *The Great Republic*, New York: Sheed and Ward, 1942.

Isidore, St., *Etymologiarum Libri XX*, Migne, *Patres Latini*, vol. 82.

Jarrett, Bede, *Social Theories of the Middle Ages*, Boston: Little, Brown, 1926.

Jenks, Edward, *The New Jurisprudence*, London: John Murray, 1933.

Jones, R. L., *International Arbitration as a Substitute for War*, St. Andrews: University Press, 1907.

Justinian, *Digest*. English translation in S. P. Scott, *The Civil Law*, 17 vols. in 7, Cincinnati: Central Trust, 1932.

Kuhlmann, B. C., *Der Gesetzesbegriff beim hl. Thomas von Aquin in Lichte des Rechtsstudiums seiner Zeit*, Bonn: Peter Hanstein, 1912.

Lange, Christian, *Histoire de l'internationalisme, I: Jusqu'à la Paix de Westphalie* (Tome IV of "Publications de Institut Nobel Norvégien"), Kristiania: H. Aschehoug, 1919.

Laski, Harold J., *The Foundations of Sovereignty and other Essays*, New York: Harcourt, Brace, 1921.

——, *Studies in the Problem of Sovereignty*, New Haven: Yale University Press, 1917.

Lichtenberger, James P., *Development of Social Theory*, New York: Century, 1923.

Littlejohn, J. M., *The Political Theory of the Schoolmen and Grotius*, New York: Columbia University, 1896.

Lottin, Odon, *Le droit naturel chez Saint Thomas d'Aquin et ses prédécesseurs*, Bruges: Ch. Beyaert, 1931.

McDonald, William J., *The Social Value of Property according to St. Thomas Aquinas*, Washington: The Catholic University of America Press, 1939.

McIlwain, Charles H., *The Growth of Political Thought in the West*, New York: Macmillan, 1932.

McKenna, Charles H., "Vitoria and his Times," in *Francisco de Vitoria*, Addresses delivered at the Catholic University of America, May 1, 1932, Washington, 1932.

Marcus Aurelius Antoninus, *The Communings with Himself of Marcus Aurelius Antoninus*. Translation by C. R. Haines (Loeb Classical Library), New York: Putnam's, 1926.

Maritain, Jacques, *Scholasticism and Politics*, New York: Macmillan, 1940.

Meyer, Hans, *Thomas von Aquin*, Bonn: Peter Hanstein, 1938.

Meulen, Jacob Ter, *Der Gedanke der Internationalen Organisation in seiner Entwicklung*, I: 1300-1800, Haag: Martinus Nijhoff, 1917.

Michel, Suzanne, *La Notion Thomiste du Bien Commun*, Paris: J. Vrin, 1932.

Muller, A., "The Organization of International Society" in *The Foundations of International Order*, Oxford: Catholic Social Guild, 1938.

Müller, Josef, *Das Friedenswerk der Kirche in den letzten drei Jahrhunderten* (1598-1917), Berlin: Deutsche Verlagsgesellschaft für Politik und Geschichte, 1927.

Murphy, Edward F., *St. Thomas' Political Doctrine and Democracy*, Washington: The Catholic University of America, 1921.

Nys, Ernest, *Les origines du droit international*, Brussels: Alfred Castaigne, 1894.

Phillipson, Coleman, *The International Law and Custom of Ancient Greece and Rome*, 2 vols., London: Macmillan, 1911.

Pitt, Felix, *Nationalism*, Fribourg: University of Fribourg, 1933.

du Plessis, Jean, *The Human Caravan*, New York: Sheed and Ward, 1939.

Plutarch, "On the Fortune or the Virtue of Alexander," in *Moralia*, vol. IV. Translation by F. C. Babbitt (Loeb Classical Library), Cambridge: Harvard University Press, 1936.

Polybius, *The Histories*. Translation by W. R. Paton (Loeb Classical Library), New York: Putnam's, 1922-1927.

Potter, P. B., *Introduction to the Study of International Organization*, New York: Century, 1922.

Prudentius, *Contra Symmachum*, Migne, *Patres Latini*, vol. 60.

Ramsay, Sir W. M., *The Imperial Peace—An Ideal in European History*, Oxford: At the Clarendon Press, 1913.

Redslob, Robert, *Histoire des grandes principes du droit des gens*, Paris: Rousseau, 1923.

———, *Théorie de la Société des Nations*, Paris: Rousseau, 1927.

Regout, Robert, *La doctrine de la guerre juste*, Paris: A. Pedone, 1935.

Renard, Georges, *La théorie de l'institution*, premier volume, Paris: Recueil Sirey, 1930.

———, "Les fondements philosophiques du droit international," in *Les grandes activités de la Société des Nations devant la pensée Chrétienne*, Paris: Editions Spes, 1932.

Roland-Gosselin, Bernard, *La doctrine politique de Saint Thomas d'Aquin*, Paris: Marcel Riviere, 1928.

Rolbiecki, John J., *The Political Philosophy of Dante Alighieri*, Washington: The Catholic University of America, 1922.

Rommen, H., *Die Staatslehre des Franciscus Suarez, S.J.*, Munich: M. Gladbach, 1926.

Rostovtseff, Michael, "International Relations in the Ancient World," in Walsh, E. A., *The History and Nature of International Relations*, New York: Macmillan, 1922.

Ryan, John A., "Christian Principles of War and Peace," in *Declining Liberty and Other Papers*, New York: Macmillan, 1927.

Ryan, John A., and Francis J. Boland, *Catholic Principles of Politics*, New York: Macmillan, 1940.

Ryan, John K., *Modern War and Basic Ethics*, Milwaukee: Bruce, 1940.

Schilling, Otto, *Der Staats-und Soziallehre des hl. Thomas von Aquin*, Paderborn: Ferdinand Schöningh, 1923.

Schücking, Walther, *Die Organisation der Welt*, Leipzig: Alfred Kröner, 1909.

Schwalm, R. P., *Leçons de Philosophie Sociale*, Paris: Bloud, 1910.

Schwer, Wilhelm, *Catholic Social Theory*, St. Louis: Herder, 1940.

Scott, James Brown, "Development of Diplomacy in Modern Times," in Walsh, E. A., *The History and Nature of International Relations*, New York: Macmillan, 1922.

———, *Law, the State, and the International Community*, 2 vols., New York: Columbia University Press, 1939.

———, *The Catholic Conception of International Law*, Washington: Georgetown University Press, 1934.

———, *The Spanish Origin of International Law, Part I: Francisco de Vitoria and His Law of Nations*, Publication of the Carnegie Endowment for International Peace in "Classics of International Law" Series, Oxford: At the Clarendon Press, 1934.

———, "Vitoria and International Law," in *Francisco de Vitoria*, Addresses delivered at the Catholic University of America, May 1, 1932, Washington, 1932.

Seneca, Lucius Annaeus, *De Otio*, in *Moral Essays*, vol. II. Translation by J. W. Basore (Loeb Classical Library), New York: Putnam's, 1928.

Sheen, Fulton J., *Whence Come Wars*, New York: Sheed and Ward, 1940.

Stawell, Florence M., *Growth of International Thought*, New York: Henry Holt, 1930.

Stratmann, Franciskus, *The Church and War*, London: Sheed and Ward, 1928.

Sturzo, Luigi, *Church and State*, New York: Longmans, Green, 1939.

———, *The International Community and the Right of War*, London: George Allen and Unwin, 1929.

Suarez, Francis, *De Legibus et Legislatore Deo*, vols. V and VI of *Opera Omnia*, Paris: Vives, 1845.

Sukiennicki, Wiktor, *La souveraineté des états en droit international moderne*, Paris: A. Pedone, 1927.

Taparelli d'Azeglio, R. P., *Essai théorique de droit naturel*, 4 vols., Paris: H. Casterman, 1857.

Thorning, Joseph, *Builders of the Social Order*, New York: Catholic Literary Guild, 1940.

Vann, Gerald, *Morality and War*, London: Burns Oates and Washbourne, 1939.

Vanderpol, A., *Le droit de guerre d'après les théologiens et les canonistes du Moyen-Age*, Paris: A. Tralin, 1911.

———, *La doctrine scolastique du droit de guerre*, Paris: A. Pedone, 1925.

Vitoria, Francisco de, *Comentarios a la Secunda Secundae de Santo Tomás*, in "Biblioteca de Teólogos Españoles," edited by R. P. Vincente Beltrán de Heredia, O.P., Salamanca, 1932-1935.

———, *Relectiones Theologicae XII*, Salamanca: Apud Joannes à Canova, 1565.

———, *De Indis (De Indis recenter inventis relectio prior)*. Translation by John P. Bate.

———, *De Jure Belli (De Indis, sive de iure belli Hispanorum in barbaros, relectio posterior)*. Translation by John P. Bate.

———, *De Potestate Civili*. Translation by Gwladys L. Williams.

———, *De Potestate Ecclesiae*. Translation by Gwladys L. Williams (Part I, sect. v.). The translations of the above four *Relectiones* are contained as Appendices in Scott, J. B., *The Spanish Origin of International Law, Part 1: Francisco de Vitoria and His Law of Nations*, Oxford: At the Clarendon Press, 1934. The first two are also contained in a special edition entitled: Vitoria, *De Indis et de iure belli relectiones, Being Parts of Relectiones theologicae XII*, in "Classics of International Law," Washington: Carnegie Institution, 1917.

Walker, Thomas A., *A History of the Law of Nations*, 2 vols., Cambridge: At the University Press, 1899.

Walsh, Edmund A., *The History and Nature of International Relations*, New York: Macmillan, 1922.

Wilson, Florence, *The Origins of the League Covenant*, London: Hogarth Press, 1928.

Wright, Herbert Francis, *Francisci de Vitoria de Iure Belli Relectio*, Washington: The Catholic University of America, 1916.

———, "Vitoria and the State," in *Francisco de Vitoria*, Addresses delivered at the Catholic University of America, May 1, 1932, Washington, 1932.

Wright, R. F., *Medieval Internationalism*, London: Williams and Morgate, 1930.

de Wulf, Maurice, *Philosophy and Civilization in the Middle Ages*, Princeton: Princeton University Press, 1922.

York, Elizabeth, *Leagues of Nations, Ancient, Medieval and Modern*, London: The Swarthmore Press, 1919,

Zeiller, Jacques, *L'idée de l'état dans Saint Thomas d' Aquin*, Paris: Felix Alcan, 1910.

PAPAL DOCUMENTS, PAMPHLETS, PERIODICALS

America's Peace Aims, Washington: The Catholic Association for International Peace, 1941.

Bésiade, Th., "L'ordre social," *Revue des sciences philosophiques et théologiques*, vol. XIII, 1924, pp. 5-19.

Butler, Nicholas Murray, *The Everlasting Conflict*, Address delivered at the 185th Commencement of Columbia University, June 6, 1939.

———, *Toward a Federal World*, Address delivered at the Parrish Art Museum, Southampton, Long Island, September 3, 1939.

Cartwright, John K., "Contributions of the Papacy to International Peace," *Catholic Historical Review*, new series vol. VIII, April 1928, pp. 157-168.

Cathrein, Victor, "Das jus gentium im römischen Recht und beim hl. Thomas von Aquin," *Philosophisches Jahrbuch*, vol. II, 1889, pp. 373-388.

Cole, Charles W., "International Economic Interdependence," *International Conciliation*, no. 369, April 1941, pp. 240-245.

Delos, J. T., "La société internationale au regard du droit naturel" *Revue des sciences philosophiques et théologiques*, vol. XV, 1926, pp. 145-160.

———, Review of Rommen, H., *Die Staatslehre des Franz Suarez, S.J.*, in *Bulletin Thomiste*, vol. VI, March 1929, pp. 490-496.

———, Review of Renard, G., *La théorie de l'Institution*, in *Bulletin Thomiste*, vol. VIII, January 1931, pp. 207-209.

Emmanuel, Cyprian, *The Ethics of War*, Washington: The Catholic Association for International Peace, 1932.

———, *The Morality of Conscientious Objection to War*, Washington: The Catholic Association for International Peace, 1941.

Farrell, Walter, "Natural Foundations of the Political Philosophy of St. Thomas," *Proceedings of the Seventh Annual Meeting of the American Catholic Philosophical Association*, 1931, pp. 75-85.

Eppstein, John, *A Catholic Looks at the League*, Oxford: Catholic Social Guild, 1937.

Fenwick, Charles G., *Arbitration and the World Court*, Washington: The Catholic Association for International Peace, 1937.

————, *A Primer of Peace*, Washington: The Catholic Association for International Peace, 1937.

Gemmel, J., "Die Justitia in der Lehre des hl. Thomas," *Scholastik*, vol. XII, 1937, pp. 204-228.

Gerig, Benjamin, "An Appraisal of the League of Nations," *International Conciliation*, no. 369, April 1941, pp. 303-316.

Hayes, Carlton J. H., "Nationalism," *International Conciliation*, no. 369, April 1941, pp. 227-239.

————, *Patriotism, Nationalism, and the Brotherhood of Man*, Washington: The Catholic Association for International Peace, 1937.

Krey, A. C., "The International State of the Middle Ages: Some Reasons for its Failure," *American Historical Review*, vol. XXVIII, October 1922, pp. 1-12.

Larequi, J., "Del 'jus gentium' al Derecho internacional. Francesco de Vitoria y los teólogos españoles del siglo XVI," *Razón y Fe*, vol. LXXXIII, 1928, pp. 21-37.

Laversin, M. J., "Droit naturel et droit positif d'après saint Thomas," *Revue Thomiste*, new series, vol. XVI, 1933, pp. 3-49; 177-216.

McIlwain, Charles H., "A Fragment on Sovereignty," *Political Science Quarterly*, vol. XLVIII, 1933, pp. 94-106.

McKenna, C. H., *Francis de Vitoria*, Washington: The Catholic Association for International Peace, 1930.

————, "Francis de Vitoria, the Founder of International Law," *Dominicana*, vol. XIV, December 1929, pp. 291-297.

MacLean, Donald A., *The Permanent Peace Program of Pope Benedict XV*, Washington: The Catholic Association for International Peace, 1931.

Maddox, William P., *European Plans for World Order*, Philadelphia: The American Academy of Political and Social Science, 1940.

Nettleship, Henry, "Ius Gentium" *The Journal of Philology*, vol. XIII, 1885, pp. 169-181.

O'Donnell, Charles (editor) *The World Society*, Washington: The Catholic Association for International Peace, 1941.

Pfeiffer, Nicholaus, "Doctrinae Iuris Internationalis iuxta Franciscum de Vitoria, O.P., Celeberrrimum Studiorum D. Thomae saeculo XVI Restauratorem," *Xenia Thomistica*, vol. III, 1925, pp. 391-421.

Pope Benedict XV, *Ad Beatissimi*, Nov. 1, 1914.

————, Allocution of August 1, 1917—*Letter to the Leaders of the Belligerent Nations*.

————, *Pacem Dei Munus Pulcherrimum*, May 23, 1920.

Pope Leo XIII, *Aeterni Patris*, Aug. 4, 1879.

————, *Immortale Dei*, Nov. 1, 1885.

————, *Sapientiae Christianae*, Jan. 10, 1890.

Pope Pius XI, *Ubi Arcano Dei*, Dec. 23, 1922.

———, *Studiorum Ducem*, June 29, 1923.

———, *Quas Primas*, Dec. 11, 1925.

———, Allocution of December 24, 1930.

———, *Quadragesimo Anno*, May 15, 1931.

———, *Caritate Christi Compulsi*, May 3, 1932.

———, *Divini Redemptoris*, March 19, 1937.

Pope Pius XII, *Summi Pontificatus*, October 20, 1939.

———, Christmas Message, Dec. 24, 1939.

Pope Benedict XV and Pope Pius XI: Appeals for Peace, Washington: The Catholic Association for International Peace.

Peace Action of Pope Benedict XV, Washington: The Catholic Association for International Peace.

Peace Statements by Recent Popes, Washington: The Catholic Association for International Peace, 1930.

Pius XII and Peace, Washington: The National Catholic Welfare Conference, 1940.

Rappard William E., "Du Fédéralisme International," *L'Esprit International*, no. 53, Jan. 1940, pp. 1-22.

Renard, R. G., "Thomisme et droit social," *Revue des sciences philosophiques et théologiques*, vol. XXIII, 1934, pp. 40-81.

Robinson, Pascal, "Peace Laws and Institutions of the Mediaeval Church," *Ecclesiastical Review*, vol. LII, May 1915, pp. 523-536.

Roemer, W. F., "St. Thomas and the Ethical Basis of International Law," *Proceedings of the Third Annual Meeting of the American Catholic Philosophical Association*, 1927, pp. 102-112.

Roemer, W. F., and J. T. Ellis, *The Catholic Church and Peace Efforts*, Washington: The Catholic Association for International Peace, 1934.

Ruyssen, Th., "De quelques difficultés du fédéralisme international," *L'Esprit International*, no. 54, April 1940, pp. 226-235.

———, "Le droit des peuples a disposer d'eux-mêmes," *Revue de metaphysique et morale*, vol. XXXIX, 1932, pp. 471-501.

Ryan, John A. and others, *International Ethics*, Washington: The Catholic Association for International Peace, 1928.

———, *International Economic Life*, Washington: The Catholic Association for International Peace, 1934.

———, *Obligations of Catholics to Promote Peace* and *The Rights of Peoples*, Washington: The Catholic Association for International Peace, 1940.

Schaefer, Mary Catherine, *Catholic Organization for Peace in Europe*, Washington: The Catholic Association for International Peace, 1935.

——, *A Papal Mosaic*, Washington: The Catholic Association for International Peace, 1936.

Syllabus on International Relations, Washington: The Catholic Association for International Peace, 1937.

Tonneau, J., "La Société international et les principes de droit public," *Revue Thomiste*, vol. XIII, 1930, pp. 401-414.

——, Book Review in *Bulletin Thomiste*, vol. XII, July-Sept. 1935, pp. 498-499.

Tourscher, F. E., *War and Peace in St. Augustine's de Civitate Dei*, Washington: The Catholic Association for International Peace, 1934.

Wright, Herbert Francis, "St. Augustine and International Peace," *Thought*, vol. V, Dec. 1931, pp. 399-416.

——, "The 'De Potestate Civili' of Vitoria," *Proceedings of the Seventh Annual Meeting of the American Catholic Philosophical Association*, 1931, pp. 85-95.

——, "International Law: Old Wine in New Bottles," *The Catholic World*, vol. CXXXII, Feb. 1931, pp. 513-521.

——, "A Sixteenth Century Theologian and International Law," *The Catholic World*, vol. CV, July 1917, pp. 457-462.

Wright, Quincy, "Fundamental Problems of International Organization," *International Conciliation*, no. 369, April 1941, pp. 468-492.

de Wulf, Maurice, "The Society of Nations in the Thirteenth Century," *International Journal of Ethics*, vol. XXIX, Jan. 1919, pp. 210-229.